PSYCHO SUP

English for psychologists

David Kerridge
Alain Lieury

DUNOD

Document et maquette de couverture
Franco Novati

ISBN 2 10 003653 X

Teacher Notes

This book has been conceived and written with the twin aims of helping the student of psychology to understand the technical texts that he/she has to encounter and to widen his/her perspectives in the study of psychology.
Most parts of the book consist of between 4 to 8 sections and deal with all the important aspects of reading comprehension. However, the book is designed to be used with flexibility; the teacher is not constrained to work through every comprehension question. But the pre-reading and certain of the vocabulary activities should be done before the text is read (this is clearly noted where appropriate). Also, many oral activities have been included (mini-presentations, meetings, interviews etc). Although these are thematically linked to the texts, they are designed to stimulate oral practice rather than to help the understanding of the texts themselves.

A few technical remarks:

— By common consent, the authors have decided to use American spelling in the comprehension questions and activities directly related to the texts (as most of them were originally published in American journals) while British spelling has been used in the other parts of the book (Activities, Grammar review etc).

— Essentials for Reading Comprehension. As this section covers large areas where many French-speaking readers encounter difficulties, it is recommended that it be covered fairly early on in the university year so as to avoid continual and repeated student "blockages".

— As you can see, no "Answer Key" has been provided in this book. For two reasons: a) it is not designed as self-study material, and b) a key to the comprehension questions would have involved an extremely voluminous appendix, running to some thirty pages.

— Finally, the Technical Glossaries. These feature explanations in French of English terms. Not only does this help the English teacher (who would, naturally, have difficulty in explaining some of the more technical words with sufficient precision) but also helps the student who will find an immediately-comprehensible explanation of such terms. In other words, bearing in mind the twin emphases of this book, the authors have taken care not to raise any unnecessary linguistic barriers. (Words explained in the technical glossaries are shown in italics in the texts and followed by asterisks *)

Note : les textes de psychanalyse ont été sélectionnés et le lexique correspondant a été réalisé par François Sauvagnat, psychanalyste, maître de conférence à l'Université Rennes 2.

Contents

Part 6. Psychopathology and Psychoanalysis 125

Part 7. Biological Sciences: Biology, Neurology, Ethology... 153

Part 1

History

1

Behaviorism

John B. Watson, 1924

During the rise of scientific psychology which lasted from the middle of the nineteenth to the beginning of this century, Watson breaks definitively with the subjective psychology of introspection. He proposes an objective psychology founded on the observation of behavior. He bases himself on a consequence of the Darwinian theory which still provokes hostile reactions when stated as plainly as Watson does: that human beings are animals.

What were the first reactions to behaviorist theory, and why were they so violent?

1. Looking back over the history of the behavioristic movement since it began in overt form in 1912, it seems hard at first sight to understand why *behaviorism** has had to weather such a continuous storm.

2. Behaviorism, as I tried to develop it in my lectures at Columbia in 1912 and in my earliest writings, was an attempt to do one thing—to apply to the experimental study of man the same kind of procedure and the same language of description that many research men had found useful for so many years in the study of animals lower than man. We believed then, as we do now, that man is an animal different from other animals only in the types of behavior he displays.

3. I think the forcing of this conviction caused most of the storm. It brought out the same type of resistance that appeared when Darwin's "Origin of Species" was first published. Human beings do not want to class themselves with other animals. They are willing to admit that they are animals but "something else in addition." It is this "something else" that causes the trouble.

How does the author categorize consciousness? Does he hold it in esteem?

4. Behaviorism, on the contrary, holds that the subject matter of human psychology *is the behavior of the human being.* Behaviorism claims that consciousness is neither a definite nor a usable concept. The behaviorist, who has been trained always as an experimentalist, holds, further, that belief in the existence of consciousness goes back to the ancient days of superstition and magic.

5. The great mass of the people even today has not yet progressed very far away from savagery—it wants to believe in magic.

Is the author a religious man?

6. One example of such a religious concept is that every individual has a *soul* which is separate and distinct from the *body.*

This soul is really a part of a supreme being. This ancient view led to the philosophical platform called "dualism." This dogma has been present in human psychology from earliest antiquity. No one has ever touched a soul, or seen one in a test tube, or has in any way come into relationship with it as he has with the other objects of his daily experience. Nevertheless, to doubt its existence is to become a heretic and once might possibly even have led to the loss of one's head. Even today the man holding a public position dare not question it.

What effect did the renaissance have on man's view of the universe?

7. With the development of the physical sciences which came with the renaissance, a certain release from this stifling soul cloud was obtained. A man could think of astronomy, of the celestial bodies and their motions, of gravitation and the like, without involving soul.

Can thinking be explained in behavioristic terms?

8. The behaviorist asks: Why don't we make what we can *observe* the real field of psychology? Let us limit ourselves to things that can be observed, and formulate laws concerning only those things. Now what can we observe? We can observe *behavior —what the organism does or says.* And let us point out at once: that *saying* is doing—that is, *behaving.* Speaking overtly or to ourselves (thinking) is just as objective a type of behavior as baseball.

9. The rule, or measuring rod, which the behaviorist puts in front of him always is: Can I describe this *bit** of behavior I see in terms of "*stimulus** and response"? By stimulus we mean any object in the general environment or any change in the tissues themselves due to the physiological condition of the animal, such as the change we get when we keep an animal from sex activity, when we keep it from feeding, when we keep it from building a nest. By response we mean anything the animal does —such as turning toward or away from a light, jumping at a sound, and more highly organized activities such as building a skyscraper, drawing plans, having babies, writing books, and the like.

10. Behaviorism, as you have already grasped from our preliminary discussion, is, then, a natural science that takes the whole field of human adjustments as its own. Its closest scientific companion is physiology. Indeed you may wonder, as we proceed, whether behaviorism can be differentiated from that science. It is different from physiology only in the grouping of its problems, not in fundamentals or in central viewpoint. Physiology is particularly interested in the functioning of parts of the animal—for example, its digestive system, the circulatory system, the nervous system, the excretory systems, the mechanics of neural and muscular response. Behaviorism, on the other hand, while it is intensely interested in all of the functioning of these parts, is intrinsically interested in what the whole animal will do from morning to night and from night to morning.

What is the main task of the behaviorist psychologist and what must she/ he do to accomplish this task?

11. The interest of the behaviorist in man's doings is more than the interest of the spectator—he wants to control man's reactions as physical scientists want to control and manipulate other natural phenomena. It is the business of behavioristic psychology to be able to predict and to control human activity.

To do this it must gather scientific data by experimental methods. Only then can the trained behaviorist predict, given the stimulus, what reaction will take place; or, given the reaction, state what the situation or stimulus is that has caused the reaction.

Exercises 1

1. *Speed reading*

After reading, note down the answers to the following :

- *Paragraph 2 :* In what way is man different from other animals?
- *Paragraph 6 :* How is "dualism" defined?
- *Paragraph 8 :* What is the author's definition of "behavior"?
- *Paragraph 9 :* Give an example of an animal's "response".
- *Paragraph 10 :* How is behaviorism different from physiology?

2. *Vocabulary*

From the context, try to guess the meaning of the following as they are used in the text :

- *Paragraph 1 :* to weather a storm
- *Paragraph 2 :* to display
- *Paragraph 4 :* to hold
- *Paragraph 6 :* a soul
- *Paragraph 6 :* a test tube
- *Paragraph 8 :* to point out
- *Paragraph 10 :* to grasp
- *Paragraph 11 :* to gather

3. *Grammar review*

- **Reference words**

As their name suggests, these words refer back (or more rarely, forward) to other words or concepts in a text. Their function is to make the text "lighter", more readable.

Look at this example :

"John ate his breakfast. John ate his breakfast quickly because he was late."

This can be improved :

"John ate his breakfast in the kitchen. He ate it quickly because he was late."

"He" and "it" are reference words.
However, the referents are not always so easy to locate.

a. Now read the following extracts from the text. What do the underlined words refer to?

– One example of such a religious concept is that every individual has a soul which is separate and distinct from the body.
– No one has ever touched a soul, or seen one in a test tube, or has in any way come into relationship with it as he has with the other objects of his daily experience. Nevertheless, to doubt its existence is to become a heretic and once might possibly even have led to the loss of one's head. Even today the man holding a public position dare not question it.
– Behaviorism, as you have already grasped from our preliminary discussion, is, then, a natural science that takes the whole field of human adjustments as its own. Its closest scientific companion is physiology. Indeed you may wonder, as we proceed, whether behaviorism can be differentiated from that science. It is different from physiology only in the grouping of its problems, not in fundamentals or in central viewpoint.
– Behaviorism, on the other hand, while it is intensely interested in all the functioning of these parts, is intrinsically...
– It is the business of behavioristic psychology to be able to predict and to control human activity. To do this it must gather scientific data by experimental methods.

b. How can the following passage be improved by the use of reference words (which will involve some changes in punctuation)?

"Last night Roger and Mary went to a restaurant, a restaurant that was featured in the Michelin Guide. Roger and Mary had already reserved a table near the window. The window looked out onto a beautiful view of a river. Roger and Mary arrived at eight o'clock and were shown to their table by the head waiter. The head waiter gave Roger and Mary two menus and from the two menus Roger and Mary chose Roger and Mary's dinner. For dessert, Roger had a fruit salad and Mary had a fruit salad too. The bill was expensive and Roger didn't have enough money to pay the bill. There was a scandal in the restaurant. The scandal ruined Roger and Mary's evening."

4. *Between the lines*

a. Read paragraph 8 again. *What do we notice about the tone? Let's look closer.* It is friendly, almost intimate when contrasted to the preceding paragraphs. It consists of rhetorical questions (Why don't we...?) and invitations to participate (Let's...)

Transform the following sentences as above :

– It is necessary to study the discipline as a whole (invitation).
– We must limit ourselves to observable phenomena (rhetorical question).

b. Linguistic devices of this kind are much used by public speakers to emphasize the points they wish to make. Another way of emphasizing a point is by using "cleft sentences".

Look at the following sentences :
- We want better education.
- What we want is better education.

And again :
- The country needs more modern hospitals.
- It's more modern hospitals that the country needs.

Which sentences are more forceful ?

Transform these sentences as above :
- I like cowboy films best
- We must humanize clinical practices
- Central government should reform the municipalities

5. *Translation*

The following sentences are not too difficult to understand "globally". Translate them into French, taking account of the nuances :
- *Paragraph 2 :* from "Behaviorism, as I tried to develop..." to "... animals lower than man."
- *Paragraph 5 :* from "No one has ever touched ..." to "... his daily experience."
- *Paragraph 9 :* from "Behaviorism, on the other hand, ..." to "... night to morning."

6. *Spelling*

• American / British differences.

Although there are differences between British and American spelling, they are not very great and can be summarized as follows :
"Behaviorism", the title of Watson's text, would be spelt "Behaviourism" in British English.

Other words which follow a certain logic of difference are :

crueler (Am) crueller (Brit)	– in many comparative adjectives, there is no doubling of the final consonant
tire (Am) tyre (Brit)	– the "y" often becomes an "i" in this class of word
meter (Am) metre (Brit)	– British English keeps the original "re" spelling
categorize (Am) categorise (Brit)	– in this class of verb, the British "s" is replaced by "z" in American. In British English both spellings are acceptable

These rules are fairly elastic and do not affect the pronunciation of the words.

However, there is much vocabulary that is totally different in the two languages (for example "pants" in American means "trousers" in British English). But these differences should not pose many problems for comprehension or specialist texts (the majority of which are American).

7. *Activity*

Form into pairs or small groups and read about the following – conflictual – situation :

The government of Pitrovia plans to build a new prison in the vicinity of the village of Angbridge, the birthplace of Pitrovia's national poet Petrony Makepeace. Angbridge is one of the main tourist attractions of Pitrovia and draws 20 000 visitors a month between May and September. But in the winter months Angbridge is deserted, except by its permanent residents, most of whom are fairly old. The younger villagers are obliged to seek seasonal work in the capital of Pitrovia or to register as unemployed.

Arguments for the prison	*Arguments against the prison*
- provide winter employment	- discourage the tourists
- far from city centres	- frighten the villagers
- only non-violent offenders	- prison guards low-paid
- provide cheap apprentice labour	- destroy spirit of village
- allow village development grants	- vulgar idea - Makepeace was hung for treason

You and your partner(s) are local councillors. It is a public meeting. One supports and the other(s) oppose the scheme. Prepare your arguments along the lines suggested, adding any ideas of your own. Now debate the problem. Do not hesitate to be demagogic.

8. *Discussion*

a. Read the last paragraph of Watson's text again, especially the sentence : "It is the business of behavioristic psychology to be able to predict and to control human activity." Bearing in mind that this text was written in 1924, how do you think the idea of "controlling" human activity has evolved ? Or has it not changed ?

b. If this text had been written today, would it be the same ? If not, which of Watson's ideas would be different ?

9. *Translate into English*

Le Behaviorisme est un courant historique dépassé aujourd'hui mais qui reste pour le psychologue scientifique comme une référence de départ. Watson exagérait lorsque, dans son style énergique, il supprimait du vocabulaire scientifique tous les termes hérités de la philosophie : image, langage, mémoire et même conscience. Mais il faut se rappeler que la psychologie expérimentale, née en Allemagne de la physiologie sensorielle, n'avait pas rompu avec la méthode philosophique, l'introspection. Par ailleurs, sans Watson, la psychologie serait restée très humaniste avec la croyance que l'homme n'est à aucun degré comparable à l'animal parce qu'il a une âme. Cet état d'esprit persiste en pédagogie par exemple, où l'on entend que l'esprit n'est pas mesurable. C'est probablement l'impact plus grand du behaviorisme aux Etats-Unis et en Angleterre et l'influence plus persistante de l'humanisme philosophique en France qui ont fait que les études expérimentales en Education se sont développées dans les pays anglo-saxons tandis que l'Education en France est le plus souvent basée sur l'introspection ou le discours philosophique.

2

Cybernetics

Norbert Wiener, November1948

The technological development during the second world war led to the creation of sciences derived from electronics. Norbert Wiener proposed a new pluridisciplinary science, "cybernetics" which englobed machine systems as well as living systems. This science anticipated considerable developments with a new terminology that had to be invented (eg "cognitic"). This terminology was necessary when attempting to define the interactive relations: psychology and computers, the perspective of information processing, cognitive sciences and artificial intelligence. Some observers, not having understood this perspective, considered the psychologists to be simple-minded in their attempts to assimilate the brain and the computer. However, already Wiener was using the analogics in both senses (see Part 8). In the chosen extracts, Wiener anticipated certain key ideas which would be developed ten or twenty years later. The security of the functioning of a large system can be ensured not by long stages of verification but by the multiplication of mechanisms which leads to a vicariance of the processes (developed contemporaneously by Maurice Reuchlin, as an origin of individual differences). The second important anticipation was the explanation of forgetting, (memory-lapse) in this case the affective forgetting observed by Freud brought about by the lack of accessibility in the permanent memory. This second example shows that the cybernetic perspective does not necessarily exclude pathological psychology of affectivity. Similarly, the contemporary perspective of information processing should not be limited to psychology which is exclusively "cognitive".

The concept of cybernetics has disappeared, probably a victim of its own success. It has split into several different sciences—computer sciences, robotics, bionics and "cognitics"—but the pluridisciplinary spirit of cybernetics is still present in the perspective of information processing.

Cybernetics englobes the human brain with a machine. (True / False)

The ambitions of cybernetics are wide. (True / False)

1. Cybernetics is a word invented to define a new field in science. It combines under one heading the study of what in a human context is sometimes loosely described as thinking and in engineering is known as control and communication. In other words, cybernetics attempts to find the common elements in the functioning of automatic machines and of the human nervous system, and to develop a theory which will cover the entire field of control and communication in machines and in living organisms.

What brain functions can the machine simulate?

2. It is well known that between the most complex activities of the human brain and the operations of a simple adding machine there is a wide area where brain and machine overlap. In their more elaborate forms, modern *computing machines** are capable of memory, association, choice and many other brain functions. Indeed, the experts have gone so far in the elaboration of such machines that we can say the human brain behaves very much like the machines. The construction of more and more complex mechanisms actually is bringing us closer to an understanding of how the brain itself operates.

3. The word cybernetics is taken from the Greek *kybernetes*, meaning steersman.

In which areas can cybernetics help?

4. The new approach represented by cybernetics—an integration of studies which is not strictly biological or strictly physical, but a combination of the two—has already given evidence that it may help to solve many problems in engineering, in physiology and very likely psychiatry.

Dr. Rosenblueth and the author believe in breaking down scientific barriers. What are these barriers? And how do they hope to proceed?

5. This work represents the outcome of a program undertaken jointly several years ago by the writer and Arturo Rosenblueth, then of the Harvard Medical School and now of the National Institute of Cardiology of Mexico. Dr. Rosenblueth is a physiologist; I am a mathematician. For many years Dr. Rosenblueth and I had shared the conviction that the most fruitful areas for the growth of the sciences were those which had been neglected as no-man's lands between the various established fields. Dr. Rosenblueth always insisted that a proper exploration of these blank spaces on the map of science could be made only by a team of scientists, each a specialist but each possessing a thoroughly sound acquaintance with the fields of his fellows.

The brain does not usually make important mistakes. (True / False)

The chance of computational error is small. (True / False)

6. These begin with perhaps the simplest question of all: how the brain avoids gross blunders or gross miscarriages of activity due to the malfunction of individual parts. Similar questions referring to the computing machine are of great practical importance, for here a chain of operations, each of which covers only a fraction of a millionth of a second, may last a matter of hours or days. It is quite possible for a chain of computational operations to involve a billion separate steps. Under these circumstances, the chance that at least one operation will go amiss is far from negligible, even though the reliability of modern electronic apparatus has exceeded the most sanguine expectations.

Why is the error-checking method clumsy with a high-speed machine?

7. In ordinary computational practice by hand or by desk machines, it is the custom to check every step of the computation and, when an error is found, to localize it by a backward process starting from the first point where the error is noted. To do this with a high-speed machine, the check must proceed at the pace of the original machine, or the whole effective order of speed of the machine will conform to that of the slower process of checking.

How do more modern methods of checking differ?

8. A much better method of checking, and in fact the one generally used in practice, is to refer every operation simultaneously to two or three separate mechanisms. When two such

Why is having "three mechanisms" important?

mechanisms are used, their answers are automatically collated against each other; and if there is a discrepancy, all data are transferred to permanent storage, the machine stops and a signal is sent to the operator that something is wrong. The operator then compares the results, and is guided by them in his search for the malfunctioning part, perhaps a tube which has burned out and needs replacement. If three separate mechanisms are used for each stage, there will practically always be agreement between two of the three mechanisms, and this agreement will give the required result. In this case the collation mechanism accepts the majority report, and the machine need not stop. There is a signal, however, indicating where and how the minority report differs from the majority report. If this occurs at the first moment of discrepancy, the indication of the position of the error may be very precise.

Messages are given to one neurone. (True / False)

9. It is conceivable, and not implausible, that at least two of the elements of this process are also represented in the nervous system. It is hardly to be expected that any important message is entrusted for transmission to a single neurone, or that an important operation is entrusted to a single neuronal mechanism. Like the computing machine, the brain probably works on a variant of the famous principle expounded by Lewis Carroll in *The Hunting of the Snark:* "What I tell you three times is true."

Information channels do not connect with each other. (True / False)

10. It is also improbable that the various channels available for the transfer of information generally go from one end of their course to the other without connecting with one another. It is much more probable that when a message reaches a certain level of the nervous system, it may leave that point and proceed to the next by one or more alternative routes. There may be parts of the nervous system, especially in the cortex, where this interchangeability is much limited or abolished. Still, the principle holds, and it probably holds most clearly for the relatively unspecialized cortical areas which serve the purpose of association and of what we call the higher mental functions.

11. So far we have been considering errors in performance that are normal, and pathological only in an extended sense. Let us now turn to those that are much more clearly pathological.

How does the combination "structure, instructions and operations" relate to the human brain?

12. This distinction between functional and organic disorders is illuminated by the consideration of the computing machine. It is not the empty physical structure of the computing machine that corresponds to the brain—to the adult brain, at least—but the combination of this structure with the instructions given it at the beginning of a chain of operations and with all the additional stored and gained from outside in the course of its operation.

"Diseases of memory". How does the author integrate this idea?

13. There is therefore nothing surprising in considering the functional mental disorders fundamentally as diseases of memory, of the circulating information kept by the brain in active state and of the long-time permeability of synapses.

Can pharmaceutical remedies be prescribed for damage to the permanent memory?

14. In long-established cases of mental disorder, the permanent memory is as badly deranged as the circulating memory. We do not seem to possess any purely pharmaceutical or surgical

Psychoanalysis can help in treating damage to the permanent memory. (True / False)

Stored information is readibly accessible. (True / False)

Why is introspection judged insufficient? How does the author describe the minimum aim of the psychoanalist in relation to hidden memories?

weapon for intervening selectively in the permanent memory. This is where psychoanalysis and the other psychotherapeutic measures come in.

15. Whether psychoanalysis is taken in the orthodox Freudian sense or in the modified senses of Jung and of Adler, or whether the psychotherapy is not strictly psychoanalytic at all, the treatment is clearly based on the concept that the stored information of the mind lies on many levels of accessibility. The effect and accessibility of this stored information are vitally conditioned by affective experiences that we cannot always uncover by introspection. The technique of the psychoanalyst consists in a series of means to discover and interpret these hidden memories, to make the patient accept them for what they are, and thus to modify, if not their content, at least the affective tone they carry, and make them less harmful.

Scientific American, November 1948

Exercises 1

1. *Vocabulary*

You probably know several of the following words and expressions, but try to guess what they mean in the context of the text:

Paragraph 1 : loosely
Paragraph 2 : to overlap
Paragraph 3 : very likely
Paragraph 5 : fruitful
Paragraph 5 : sound
Paragraph 6 : a matter of
Paragraph 6 : sanguine
Paragraph 8 : discrepancy
Paragraph 8 : tube
Paragraph 9 : it is hardly to be expected...
Paragraph 14 : to come in
Paragraph 15 : harmful

Note : "steersman" means "guide" or "controller" in this context.

2. *Grammar review*

- **The Passive**

Use of the passive voice is common in specialist texts, especially in the description of processes. To see why this is, look at the following sentence :

The technician repairs the photocopier.

It is a perfectly standard (if somewhat uninteresting) sentence, containing subject, verb and object.
However, it can be improved :

The photocopier is repaired.

Why is this second version more acceptable ? Basically because it is the technician's job to repair the photocopier, thus his presence in the sentence is superfluous, it may be "understood".
(If the original sentence had read : "The managing director repaired the photocopier", use of the passive would perhaps have been less justified).

The passive is formed as follows :

A	B	C
The surgeon	performs	the operation

A) The object becomes subject
B) The active verb is preceded by the appropriate form of "be" and transformed to its past participle
C) The subject becomes agent or is omitted completely

The operation	is performed	(by the surgeon)

• Note how the verb "be" is conjugated and the almost unlimited tense variations :
- The car is mended
- Washing machines are quickly repaired
- The woman was miraculously cured in three weeks
- Data will only be processed tomorrow
- If you ask me, he should have been given the death penalty

etc.

a. Read paragraph 8 of the text, underlining the passive verbs.
b. Transform these sentences into the passive. (Be careful, one of them does not lend itself to the passive).
- The dog ate the food
- The audience appreciated the new opera
- Peter cleans the machines every week
- He will type the letter
- They ought to introduce compulsory testing
- The porters would have packed the bags yesterday, but they forgot
- John lived in Ivy Road
- You can cross the lake by ferry

3. *Between the lines*

a. Read paragraphs 9 and 10 of the text again. The author's tone is tentative, he is making hypotheses rather than stating truths. Underline the words/expressions he uses to emphasize the tentative nature of his themes.

b. Now rewrite these paragraphs as if you were stating certainties. Check in the Modal Verbs section of Essentials for Reading comprehension (appendix).

4. *Translate into English*

Quoique le terme de cognitif ait été introduit depuis plusieurs dizaines d'années par Piaget et Bruner, il a acquis ces dernières années une valeur générique pour désigner les recherches portant sur les structures mentales, spécialement dans la perspective du traitement de l'information. La psychologie cognitive est devenue un secteur carrefour entre les psychologues et les ingénieurs ou chercheurs en informatique, et technologies nouvelles ; des équipes de recherche ou des centres de recherche cognitive sont de plus en plus nombreux à se créer.

5. *Activity*

In the author's viewpoint, "levels of accessibility of information in the memory" are clearly important. In groups of three or four, research and prepare a formal presentation of this problem from a psychological, general, social or psychoanalytical point of view. (Or you may prefer to link your presentation to the research of someone else who has worked in this field).

Text A

Physical gestalten

By Wolfgang Köhler, 1938

Behaviorism imposed itself on scientific psychology to the point of becoming the only reference. But on their arrival in the United States, German psychologists brought with them a new way of thinking inspired by Germany's highly-advanced technology—physics.

(Do exercises 1 and 2 before reading the text.)

1. When spatial, visual, auditory and intellectual processes are such as to display properties other than could be derived from the parts in summation, they may be regarded as unities illustrating what we mean by the word "*Gestalten**".

What is the difference between a single electric circuit and several of them?

2. Thus an electric circuit is a physical system precisely because the conditions prevailing at any given point are determined by those obtained in all the other parts. Contrariwise, a group of electrical circuits completely insulated from each other constitutes a complex of independent, single systems. This complex is a "whole" *only* in the mind of one who chances to think of it as such; from the physical standpoint it is a summation of independent entities.

What has been the accepted theory on sense stimuli up to now?

3. Now, although these facts are obviously familiar to physicists, they are often neglected in the theoretical treatment of biological problems. An example from the psychophysiology of space perception will illustrate this: when a number of stimuli act on different points of the sense organ at the same time, it has been the custom to interpret the action of each stimulus separately, and the total process has been considered a summation of the elementary processes which each stimulus would have aroused. A visual perception was thus physiologically ascribed to a mosaic of local nervous excitations in the visual cortex, each excitation corresponding to a single stimulus point on the retina and a single point of the object in space. Even Helmhotz proceeded in sense physiology upon this presupposition, although it is clear that the nervous system would have to satisfy very special conditions to make such a view tenable—namely, the nervous system could not be *a single physical system.*

Is this theory still valid?

4. For a time this method of treatment seemed adequate but, with the progress of psychology, difficulties began to appear which could not be covered up by the introduction of "psychological" hypotheses. And it was essentially this which led V. Ehrenfels to raise the "*Gestalt*" problem.

What do "optical illusions" demonstrate?

5. If, in the case of vision, we assume that each physically isolable stimulus produces an independent optical excitation, the *problem*, then, is to explain the unity of visual experience. As so-called optical illusions show, we do not see individual fractions of a thing; instead, the mode of appearance of each part depends not only upon the stimulation arising at *that* point but upon the conditions prevailing at other points as well. Since this fact does not bear out the assumption of isolated excitations, its explanation has been sought in terms of "*higher mental processes**". And yet, had it not been for this assumption, probably no one would have thought to maintain that visual "Gestalten" occur only as products of mental activity. The *real* assumption, of course, was that to be scientific one had to treat wholes as bare aggregates.

Printed in Great Britain by
Lowe & Brydone (Printers) Ltd, London
First published 1938

1. *Comprehension*

Read paragraph 1 only, then fill in the following—simplified—definition of Gestalt :

The .... is .... than the .... of its ....

2. *Vocabulary*

Before reading the whole text, choose the best definitions of the following verbs :

- to prevail
  a) to exist
  b) to happen
  c) to vanquish
- to bear out
  a) to cancel
  b) to support
  c) to emphasize
- to arouse
  a) to calm
  b) to negate
  c) to excite
- to be sought in
  a) to be annulled by
  b) to be saved by
  c) to be searched for
- to ascribe to
  a) to explain by
  b) to disprove with
  c) to demonstrate by

3. *Comprehension*

Now answer the following True / False questions with reference to the text.

a) The electric circuit is a physical system because its prevailing conditions are independent. *True/False*
b) The idea of a "complex" as a whole is subjective. *True/False*
c) It has been the custom to consider space perception as the totality of separate retinal stimuli. *True/False*

d) Our mode of seeing an object is dependent on the "whole" of the object. *True/False*
e) When we "perceive" something, we "think". *True/False*

Text B

The Mathematics of Communication

Warren Weaver, July 1949

The development of electronics also provoked an upsurge in communications (notably telephonic) which led to reflections on the nature of this communication so easily transformable into electrical impulses or sonic wawes. Claude Shannon and Warren Weaver (the author) have given a mathematical interpretation of information, viewed as a logarithmic function of the probability of events. This theory stimulated a great wave of the study of language, both linguistic and in psychology, and notably gave place to the statistical description of language (frequency etc.).

(question 1 should be answered before reading the text)

Having calculated the *entropy** (or the information, or the *freedom of choice**) of a certain information source, one can compare it to the maximum value this entropy could have, subject only to the condition that the source continue to employ the same symbols. The *ratio** of the actual to the maximum entropy is called the relative entropy of the source. If the relative entropy of a certain source is, say, eight-tenths, this means roughly that this source is, in its choice of symbols to form a message, about 80 per cent as free as it could possibly be with these same symbols. One minus the relative entropy is called the "*redundancy**." That is to say, this fraction of the message is unnecessary in the sense that if it were missing the message would still be essentially complete, or at least could be completed.

It is most interesting to note that the redundancy of English is just about 50 per cent. In other words, about half of the letters or words we choose in writing or speaking are under our free choice, and about half are really controlled by the statistical structure of the language, although we are not ordinarily aware of it. Incidentally, this is just about the minimum of freedom (or relative entropy) in the choice of letters that one must have to be able to construct satisfactory crossword puzzles. In a language that had only 20 per cent of freedom, or 80 per cent redundancy, it would be impossible to construct crossword puzzles in sufficient complexity and number to make the game popular.

Now since English is about 50 per cent redundant, it would be possible to save about one-half the time of ordinary telegraphy by a proper encoding process, provided one transmitted over a *noiseless channel**. When there is noise on a channel, however, there is some real advantage in not using a coding process that eliminates all of the redundancy. For the remaining redundancy helps combat the noise. It is the high redundancy of English, for example, that makes it easy to correct errors in spelling that have arisen during transmission.

Scientific American, July 1949

1. *Pre-reading activity*

Fractions and percentages and their usage in approximations.

Percentages

Look at the following diagram :

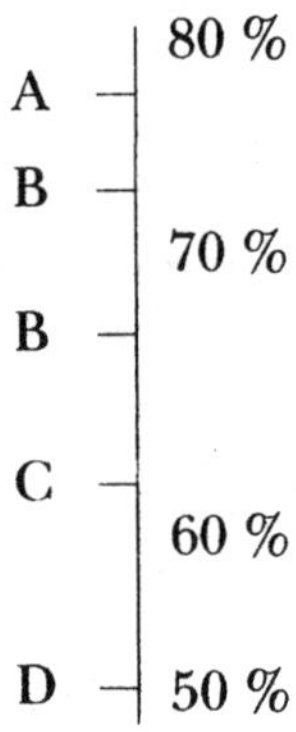

We can say :

- A is
  - ❑ coming up to
  - ❑ getting on for 80 %
  - ❑ approaching
  - ❑ nearly
- B is
  - ❑ around
  - ❑ about
  - ❑ approximately 70 %
  - ❑ roughly
- C is
  - ❑ just over
  - ❑ a bit above 60 %
- D is
  - ❑ exactly
  - ❑ precisely 50 %
  - ❑ just

Fractions

– *Note how fractions are written and spoken :*

1/4	a quarter
1/2	a half
3/4	three quarters
5/8	five eighths

– *Now re-write these sentences as "approximate fractions":*

(Example : "23 out of the 50 students failed the exam"
"Nearly half the students failed the exam.")

– The success rate was slightly lower than 1:5.
– 68 % of the educational psychologists interviewed considered they were underpaid.
– In the town of Darkmoor, unemployment rose from 1.8 to almost 3 thousand following the closure of the mines.

– *How would you write the following fractions ?*

3/5
2/3
7/8

2. *Comprehension*

Now answer these questions.

a. How is the ratio of actual to maximum entropy calculated ?
b. How does the author define redundancy in relation to relative entropy ?
c. To what degree does the statistical structure of the English language control the words we speak ?
d. Why are crossword puzzles popular in English-speaking countries ?
e. What would be the advantages of a telegraphic encoding process ?
f. Why and under what conditions is an encoding process inadvisable ?

Lexique

Behaviorism

Behaviorism est fabriqué par Watson à partir du mot "Behavior" (ou behaviour) qui signifie comportement ou conduite. Littéralement, "Behaviorism" signifie donc "Psychologie du Comportement". Le terme est importé tel quel pour entrer dans ce qu'on appelle le Franglais (et qui n'est peut-être pas à dédaigner plus que le greco-latino-gaulois qu'est le français). Au sens strict, "Behavior" est traduit par comportement et exclut les processus mentaux (ex : image mentale) ; pour se démarquer de ce behaviorisme strict, des psychologues français ont employé le terme de "conduite" en y incluant les processus mentaux. Il est donc préférable lorsqu'il y a une référence au Behaviorisme de traduire "behavior" par "comportement".

Bit : fragment ou segment

Littéralement "morceau" ou "fragment". Dans le contexte behavioriste, qui analyse le comportement comme le chimiste sous la forme d'assemblage d'unités plus petites, une traduction spécifique serait "segment" : "bit of behavior" signifie donc un segment de comportement avec l'idée qu'un comportement complexe peut s'analyser comme une séquence comportementale de plusieurs segments.

Computing machine : machine à calculer

Plus tard, a prévalu le mot "computer" (littéralement "calculateur") traduit en français par "ordinateur" puisque de telles machines font plus que de calculer.

Entropy : Entropie (Information s'est imposé)

Entropie, incertitude et information (comme l'auteur le met entre parenthèses) sont reliés puisque dans la théorie, l'information est une fonction (logarithmique) de l'incertitude (= entropie).

Freedom of choice : incertitude

Littéralement "liberté de choix" ou de façon plus technique "incertitude".

Gestalten

C'est le terme plus court de "Gestalt" qui s'est imposé. Il est difficilement traduisible d'où son importation en américain ; s'appliquant essentiellement dans le domaine de la perception, il signifie plutôt "forme" dans le sens d'une unité dont le tout n'est pas réductible à la somme de ses parties ; le terme moderne pour désigner une telle définition est "structure".

Higher mental processes : Processus mentaux supérieurs

Les premiers laboratoires de psychologie expérimentale ont étudié d'abord des processus simples, se prêtant à la mesure, seuils perceptifs et temps de réaction. En référence à ces processus sensori-moteurs inférieurs, la perception, l'intelligence, le langage, la mémoire, etc., étaient classés comme processus supérieurs. Cette distinction est tombée en désuétude car un continuum de complexité sous-tend de nombreux processus mentaux.

Noiseless channel : canal sans bruit

La théorie est née pour le téléphone et en a le vocabulaire. Les signaux électriques empruntent un canal (câble téléphonique) et les perturbations créent du "bruit" pour celui qui écoute ; dans la théorie des communications (ou de l'information) on appelle donc "bruit" (noise) toute perturbation (information supplémentaire, dégradation) du signal.

Ratio : rapport

Rapport (proportion).

Redundancy : redondance

La redondance est le supplément d'informations par rapport à la quantité minimale d'une séquence d'information.

Stimulus

Littéralement, on peut le traduire par "stimulation" ; le stimulus était l'aiguillon, branche pointue faite pour blesser les soldats ou les chevaux dans les guerres antiques ; ce terme a donc le sens d'une stimulation déclenchante d'une réaction.

Part 2

General Psychology

1

How to Teach Animals

by B. F. Skinner, December 1951

Skinner is the founder of a school of the study of learning called Operant Conditioning, which has many applications, including the well-known "Skinner's Box". This is a device used to study the conditioning of the rat (or the pigeon). In simple terms, he explains how to train domestic animals. The text may be read on two levels: either as an anecdote about how to train a dog or as a simply-described statement of the principle laws of conditioning. Some people write banalities in complicated terms, while Skinner states fundamental laws in plain language.

(Do exercise 1 before reading the text)

1. Teaching, it is often said, is an art, but we have increasing reason to hope that it may eventually become a science. We have already discovered enough about the nature of learning to devise *training techniques** which are much more effective and give more reliable results than the rule-of-thumb methods of the past. Tested on animals, the new techniques have proved superior to traditional methods of professional animal trainers; they yield more remarkable results with much less effort.

Is it possible to train an animal at home? Can laboratory conditions be replicated at home?

2. It takes rather subtle laboratory conditions to test an animal's full *learning** capacity, but the reader will be surprised at how much he can accomplish even under informal circumstances at home. Since nearly everyone at some time or other has tried, or wished he knew how, to train a dog, a cat or some other animal, perhaps the most useful way to explain the learning process is to describe some simple experiments which the reader can perform himself.

3. "Catch your rabbit" is the first item in a well-known recipe for rabbit stew. Your first move, of course, is to choose an experimental subject. Any available animal—a cat, a dog, a pigeon, a mouse, a parrot, a chicken, a pig—will do. (Children or other members of your family may also be available, but it is suggested that you save them until you have had practice with less valuable material.) Suppose you choose a dog.

What is the role of food?

4. The second thing you will need is something your subject wants, say food. This serves as a reward or—to use a term which is less likely to be misunderstood—a "*reinforcement**" for the desired behavior. Many things besides food are reinforcing—for example, simply letting the dog out for a run—but food is usually the easiest to administer in the kind of experiment to be described here. If you use food, you must of course perform the experiment when the dog is hungry, perhaps just before his dinnertime.

Can the behavior of animals be modified?

5. The reinforcement gives you a means of control over the behavior of the animal. It rests on the simple principle that whenever something reinforces a particular activity of an organism, it *increases the chances that the organism will repeat that behavior**. This makes it possible to *shape** an animal's behavior almost as a sculptor shapes a lump of clay. There is, of course, nothing new in this principle. What is new is a better understanding of the conditions under which reinforcement works best.

What is the role of the conditioned reinforcer?

6. To be effective a reinforcement must be given almost *simultaneously** with the desired behavior; a delay of even one second destroys much of the effect. This means that the offer of food in the usual way is likely to be ineffective; it is not fast enough. The best way to reinforce the behavior with the necessary speed is to use a *"conditioned" reinforcer**. This is a signal which the animal is conditioned to associate with food. The animal is always given food immediately after the *signal**, and the signal itself then becomes the reinforcer. The better the association between the two events, the better the result.

What reinforcers are suggested and what are their advantages and disadvantages?

7. For the conditioned reinforcer you need a clear signal which can be given instantly and to which the subject is sure to respond. It may be a noise or a flash of light. A whistle is not effective because of the time it takes to draw a breath before blowing it. A visual signal like a wave of the arm may not always be seen by the animal. A convenient signal is a rap on a table with a small hard object or the noise of a high-pitched device such as a "cricket."

Why must small scraps of food be used?

8. You are now ready to start the experiment with your dog. Work in a convenient place as free as possible from distraction. Let us say that you have chosen a "cricket" as your conditioned reinforcer. To build up the effect of the reinforcer begin by tossing a few scraps of food, one at a time and not oftener than once or twice a minute, where the dog may eat them. Use scraps of food so small that 30 or 40 will not greatly reduce the animal's hunger. As soon as the dog eats each scrap readily and without delay, begin to pair the cricket with the food. Sound the cricket and then toss a piece of food. Wait half a minute or so and repeat. Sound the cricket suddenly, without any preparatory movements such as reaching for food.

At what moment must reinforcement be used?

9. At this stage your subject will probably show well-marked begging behavior. It may watch you intently, perhaps jump on you, and so on. You must break up this behavior, because it will interfere with other parts of the experiment. Never sound the cricket or give food when the dog is close to you or facing you. Wait until it turns away, then reinforce. Your conditioned reinforcer is working properly when your subject turns immediately and approaches the spot where it receives food. Test this several times. Wait until the dog is in a fairly unusual position, then sound the signal. Time spent in making sure the dog immediately approaches the food will later be saved manyfold.

How, exactly, is reinforcement related to training?

10. Now, having established the noise as the reinforcer, you may begin teaching the dog. To get the feel of the technique start with some simple task, such as getting the dog to approach the handle on a low cupboard door and touch it with its nose. At first you reinforce any activity which would be part of the final completed act of approaching and touching the handle of the cupboard. The only permissible contact between you and the dog is *via* the cricket and the food. Do not touch the dog, talk to it, coax it, "draw its attention" or interfere in any other way with the experiment. If your subject just sits, you may have to begin by reinforcing any movement, however slight. As soon as the dog moves, sound the cricket and give food. Remember that your reaction time is important. Try to reinforce as nearly simultaneously with the movement as possible.

Scientific American, December 1951

Exercises 1

1. *Pre-reading activities*

a. Match the following words / expressions :

rule-of-thumb	a dish made from meat and vegetables
reliable	a material used by sculptors
stew	a small piece (of food, for example)
clay	it makes a noise
whistle	dependable
scrap	approximate

b. And now match these verbs :

to yield	to supplicate
to shape	to show
to toss	to form
to beg	to cajole
to coax	to throw

The faux ami "eventually" means :

- perhaps, at some time in the future ❑
- definitely, at some time in the future ❑
- never ❑

Note : A cricket is an insect; but in the text it means a small implement used to make a clicking noise.

2. *Grammar review*

- **Imperative verbs**

These verbs tell you what to do, give orders. In English they usually occur at or near the beginning of a sentence and are often embedded in :
– sequence formulae (First, Later..., etc.)
– expressions of cause, effect or purpose (As, To, So that..., etc.)
– conditions (If, In case of..., etc.).

– Read paragraph 8 of the text and underline all the imperative verbs.

– Now encircle the expressions linked to the imperatives and categorize them (sequence etc.).

a) Put the following sentences in order :
scraps to throw cat simultaneously meat the the of
prevent place separate order pilot in groups rooms copying in to the
recidivist counsel of case in behaviour the offender
descending the rate priority of order in responses now
calculations verify experiment but your the not results do if uneven repeat are the

b) Translate the following excerpts from the passage :
"To get the feel of the technique start with some simple task."
"Do not touch the dog, talk to it, coax it, "draw its attention" or interfere in any other way with the experiment."
"As soon as the dog moves, sound the cricket and give food."

3. *Between the lines*

Read paragraph 3 again. What tone does the author use here? And which of the following adjectives are appropriate to describe this tone?

Ironic	Serious	Pedagogical	Informal
Cruel	Pedantic	Elegaic	Sadistic

4. *Text content*

a) In your own words, define the following as used in the text:
– reinforcement
– a conditioned reinforcer
– a signal

b) Now summarize Skinner's argument using the following word-frame :

"If an organism ______________________________

____

the behavior will be repeated. A conditioned reinforcer is used to ______

____

Speed is essential in this training, so when an animal starts to perform the task ______________________________

5. *Discussion*

Does Skinner's article have implications as regards humans?

6. *Activity*

From notes, prepare a short (and not necessarily serious) oral presentation on how you would put Skinner's theory into practice to solve the following problems :
- absenteeism in a company
- graffiti in Metro stations
- schoolchildren who refuse to do their homework
- dogs that bark all night
- loud music from neighbours' appartments

Remember, the essence of Skinner's argument is that, with adequate and speedy reinforcement, an organism may be trained to modify its behaviour.

2

Eye Movements and Visual Perception

David Noton and Lawrence Stark, 1971

Following the work of such pioneers as Yarbus, who demonstrated that vision is not continuous but consists of ocular movements, Noton and Stark show how these movements function. They propose an interesting theory : the "feature ring."

(Do question 1 before reading the text)

1. Recently at the University of California at Berkeley we have developed a hypothesis about visual perception that predicts and explains this apparent regularity of *eye movement**. Essentially we propose that in the internal representation or memory of the picture the features are linked together in sequence by the memory of the eye movement required to look from one feature to the next. Thus the eyes would tend to move from feature to *feature** in a fixed order, *scanning** the picture.

2. Most of Yarbus' recordings are summaries of many *fixations** and do not contain complete information on the ordering of the fixations. Thus the regularities of eye movements predicted by our hypothesis could not be definitely confirmed from his data. To eliminate this constraint and to subject our hypothesis to a more specific test we recently made a new series of recordings of eye movements during visual perception.

3. Our subjects viewed line drawings of simple objects and abstract symbols as we measured their eye movements (using photocells to determine the movements of the "white" of the eye) and recorded them on magnetic tape. We thereby obtained a permanent record of the order of fixations made by the subjects and could play it back later at a lower speed, analyzing it at length for cycles and other regularities of movement. As in the earlier experiments, the drawings were fairly large and close to the subject's eyes, a typical drawing subtending about 20 degrees at the eye. In addition we drew the pictures with quite thin lines and displayed them with an underpowered slide projector, throwing a dim image on a screen that was fully exposed to the ordinary light in the laboratory. In this way we produced an image of low visibility and could be sure that the subject would have to look directly (foveally) at each feature that interested him, thus revealing to our recording equipment *the locus of his attention**.

4. Our initial results amply confirmed the previous impression of cycles of eye movements. We found that when a subject viewed a picture under these conditions, his eyes usually scanned it following—intermittently but repeatedly—a fixed path, which we have termed his "*scan path**" for that picture. The occurrences of the scan path were separated by periods in which the fixations were ordered in a less regular manner.

5. Each scan path was characteristic of a given subject viewing a given picture. A subject had a different scan path for every picture he viewed, and for a given picture each subject had a different scan path. A typical scan path for our pictures consisted of about 10 fixations and lasted for from three to five seconds. Scan paths usually occupied from 25 to 35 percent of the subject's viewing time, the rest being devoted to less regular eye movements.

6. It must be added that scan paths were not always observed. Certain pictures (one of a telephone, for example) seemed often not to provoke a repetitive response, although no definite common characteristic could be discerned in such pictures. The commonest reaction, however, was to exhibit a scan path.

7. This demonstration of the existence of scan paths strengthened and clarified our ideas about visual perception. In accordance with the serial hypothesis, we assume that the internal representation of an object in the memory system is an assemblage of features. To this we add a crucial hypothesis: that the features are assembled in a format we have termed a "*feature ring**". The ring is a sequence of sensory and motor *memory traces**, alternately recording a feature of the object and the eye movement required to reach the next feature. The feature ring establishes a fixed ordering of features and eye movements, corresponding to a scan path on the object.

Scientific American, 1971

Exercises 2

1. *Activity*

A telephone
is on the
the table

What does the above message say? Perhaps the following text will help to explain.

2. *Comprehension*

Read the text once quickly and, while reading, mark if the following statements are true or false (T or F)

a) Memory registers visual images with regular eye movements. (T/F)
b) Yarbus' findings do not agree with those of the authors. (T/F)
c) The subjects described the objects they were shown and their descriptions were recorded on magnetic tape. (T/F)
d) The experiments took place in a brightly-lit room. (T/F)
e) All the scan paths were different. (T/F)
f) A scan path could last up to 25 seconds. (T/F)
g) Not all the pictures provoked a "scan path response". (T/F)
h) A feature ring fixes eye movements. (T/F)

3. *Comprehension*

Now read the text again, paragraph by paragraph and answer the following questions, justifying your answers with a key word or phrase.

Para 1 : How are the features of a picture linked together?
Para 2 : In what way did Yarbus' experiments differ from those of the writers?
Para 2 : How did the writers overcome this problem?
Para 3 : Why were the subjects' eye movements recorded?
Para 3 : What was done to encourage the subjects to look directly at each picture?
Para 4 : What is a picture's "scan path"?
Para 5 : Calculate approximately for how long each picture was shown.
Para 6 : Why do you think the picture of a telephone provoked no particular scan path?
Para 7 : What new element do the authors add to their text? And how do they describe its function?

4. *Grammar review*

- **Pre-modifiers** (articles – a, an, the and the 'zero' article)

a) Read paragraph 3 from "Our subjects..." to "... of movement." Note how articles are used.

b) Now read the following text, adding appropriate pre-modifiers if and where necessary.

_______ team of dieticians and psychologists at _______ Virginia University in _______ Canada have recently made _______ series of interesting discoveries in _______ domain of _______ diet and _______ intelligence. One researcher has gone on _______ record as claiming that _______ healthy yet vitamin-supplemented diet can raise _______ child's IQ by more than twenty points.

c) How could this text be improved?

"For any but very rich, divorce was practically unobtainable in Victorian era; but even then it was much easier for husband to divorce his wife than for wife to divorce husband. Right on into sixties pejorative concept of 'matrimonial offense' remained. ... Divorce Reform Act of 1969 was claimed to be 'Casanova's Charter'.
(from "English Society since 1945", Marwick)

5. *Text content*

a) Using the following notes and appropriate link words as indicated, write a summary of the article.

Paragraph 1 : A short introduction

Paragraph 2 :

- Features linked in sequence
  - *cause/effect*
- scan picture
  - *cause/effect*
- Yarbus' recordings of ordering of fixations incomplete
  - *cause/effect*
- hypothesis not confirmed
  - *purpose*
- eliminate constraint
- new series of recordings.

Paragraph 3 :

- Subjects viewed drawings
  - *sequence*
- eye movement measured and recorded
- low-visibility image used
  - *cause/effect*
- subjects looked directly at image.

Paragraph 4 :

- Initial results showed existence of scan paths
  - *contrast*
- each scan path different.
- Internal representation of an object an assemblage of features
  - *contrast*
  - *addition*
- features formed feature ring.

Paragraph 5 :

- Definition of feature ring.

b) The article begins rather abruptly and the reference word "this" (line 4) seems to suggest that "regularity of eye movement" has already been referred to in an opening title or paragraph.
Write this title.

6. *Discussion activities*

a) Does the work done on scan paths and feature rings help to explain any problems with Activity 1?

b) Work in small groups (of 3 or 4) using full-page fairly detailed advertisements taken from some French weekly magazines. Each student takes a different advertisement then, in turn, shows it to the other group members for about one minute. Individually, the others note down what they see **in order** then compare results. Can any common scan paths be detected? (This is only a simple illustration, not a proof, as eye movements must be objectively recorded).

c) Do the authors' findings change our perceptions of art or our environment? If so, how?

Text A

Sign-gestalt or Conditioned Reflex?

Edward Chace Tolman, 1933

From the 1920s to the 1960s, Behaviorism with its associationist concepts reigned supreme. In the field of experimentation, rats were taught to function in mazes (which the associationists Watson and Hull explained in terms of conditioning). While describing himself as a behaviorist, Tolman took his inspiration from gestaltists (a paradox explained by the fact that at that time Behaviorism was thought of as "scientific psychology") and put forward the theory that behavior can be explained by superior mental mechanisms. In this perspective, he first introduced the notion of "sign-gestalt", a mental structure englobing spatial and motivational responses and information. This text is a good example of this scientific approach, the author recounting the failure of his hypothesis with humour and candour.

(Do question 1 before reading text)

The conditioned response does not mention one important thing. What is it?

The author believes there is a link between positive response stimuli and the learning process. (True/False)

1. It appears that what our *conditioned response friends** really do is to divide all responses into two sorts—positive and negative. And they argue that in a *trial and error situation** the acts which get learned are those which result in bringing the animal into the presence of further stimuli to which positive responses are already attached. And the acts which do not get learned are those which result in bringing the animal into the presence of further stimuli to which negative responses are already attached. These resultant positive and negative responses get conditioned back to the *cue stimuli**. It must be noted, however, that the positive and negative responses which thus get conditioned back may in concrete terms be as different from the original responses from which they are supposed to be derived as entering is from eating or as not-entering is from jumping back and squealing. But this last is a little point which is not stressed by the theory. Our conditioned response friends are truly both serpentish and dovelike.

In what way can the theory be useful?

The author rejects the conditioned response theory. (True/False)

2. But let us not be too captious. For it must be admitted that this conditioned response formula, even though it be thus a bit—shall we say—jesuitical, is really surprisingly workable. It can be applied usefully to most discrimination box and maze problems and, as such, it seems to provide a helpful schema for holding together past results and for predicting future ones. Nevertheless my purpose here must be to show that there are (or at any rate there ought to be) types of *maze** or *discrimination box** finding for which this all-useful though emasculated conditioned response formula will not hold.

What made the author believe that the rats would refuse to return to the food compartment?

The author used the discrimination box in an orthodox fashion (True/False)

3. By way of a first example, let me return to an experiment of my own which used a discrimination box like that just shown. After having, as part of another problem, *overtrained** rats in this discrimination box, I tried putting them directly into the food compartments and *shocking** them then and there. Then I carried them immediately around to S and started a run in the usual fashion. My assumption was that as a result of all their preceding training, in which they had been running through the box as the way to get to food, the rats would have built up what in my barbarous terminology I have called sign-gestalt expectations. These sign-gestalt expectations I assumed would be to the effect that the earlier parts of the discrimination apparatus would have become a sign or a set of signs to the rats that the encountering of the food compartments was to be achieved by running through this discrimination apparatus. And, if the rats had built up such sign-gestalt expectations, I assumed further that a single experience of the changed character of the food compartments (or, as I should put it, this changed character of the significates of the sign-gestalts) should have been enough so that upon being reintroduced to the signs (that is, to the first parts of the discrimination box) the rats would at once have inferred or remembered this new changed character in the goal compartments. And hence they should have refused to run.

What is the author's opinion of sign-gestalt expectations? Why?

The rats did not return to the food compartment (True/False)

4. But alas, no such thing. Each rat (I must confess that I tried it with only four), after having been shocked in the food compartment and then carried to the starting point, immediately dashed off gaily and just as usual through the whole discrimination apparatus and bang whack into the very food compartment in which he had just been shocked. If the rats had sign-gestalt expectations, then *sign-gestalt expectations** are not as intelligent as I have supposed them to be.

Psychological Review, May 1933

1. *Vocabulary*

Before reading the text, match these words with their definitions:

A. to stress	1. a high-pitched animal noise
B. squeal	2. happily
C. dove	3. slang – "without hesitation"
D. captious	4. a bird of peace
E. maze	5. weakened
F. emasculated	6. labyrinth
G. to infer	7. to emphasize
H. to dash off	8. to make a logical deduction
I. gaily	9. hyper-critical
J. bang whack	10. to run quickly

A	B	C	D	E	F	G	H	I	J

2. *Between the lines*

The tone of this article is :

Ironic
Aggressive
Scientific
Amusing

Find some expressions the author uses to express his attitudes.

Text B

Eye, Brain and Vision

David Hubel, 1988 (Nobel Prize 1981)

Using microelectrography, David Hubel has explored the brain of the cat and the monkey (much of his research being carried out with Wiesel). In this text he explains how, with an almost monastic patience, he recorded the bioelectric responses of neurons of visual centres, studying them one by one. Bearing in mind that the brain contains over 100 billion neurons, we can imagine that his Nobel Prize was well-deserved.

Why can't small spots of light be used?
Not all the cells respond to light stimuli in the same way. (True/False)
What must be found in the animal's brain? Why?
There are two types of light stimuli (True/False)

1. Small spots generally produce weak *responses** or none. To evoke a response, we first have to find the appropriate part of the *visual field** to stimulate, that is, the appropriate part of the screen that the animal is facing: we have to find the receptive field of the cell. It then turns out that the most effective way to influence a cell is to sweep some kind of line across the receptive field, in a direction perpendicular to the line's orientation. The line can be light on a dark background (a slit) or a dark bar on a white background or an edge boundary between dark and light. Some *cells** prefer one of these stimuli over the other two, often very strongly; others respond about equally well to all three types of stimuli. What is critical is the orientation of the line: a typical cell responds best to some optimum stimulus orientation.

What are the limitatons of present techniques of cell observation?

2. In a single experiment we can test the responses of 200 to 300 cells simply by learning all about one cell and then pushing the electrode ahead to the next cell to study it. Because once you have inserted the delicate electrode you obviously can't

Do they prevent the author from forming any conclusions?

In general, there is no measurable cell orientation preference. (True/False)

move it sideways without destroying it or the even more delicate cortex, this technique limits your examination to cells lying in a straight line. Fifty cells per millimeter of penetration is about the maximum we can get with present methods. When the orientation preferences of a few hundred or a thousand cells are examined, all orientations turn out to be about equally represented—vertical, horizontal, and every possible oblique. Considering the nature of the world we look at, containing as it does trees and horizons, the question arises whether any particular orientations, such as vertical and horizontal, are better represented than the others. Answers differ with different laboratory results, but everyone agrees that if biases do exist, they must be small—small enough to require statistics to discern them, which may mean they are negligible!

How do simple and complex cells differ?

3. In the monkey *striate cortex**, about 70 to 80 percent of cells have this property of orientation specificity. In the cat, all cortical cells seem to be orientation selective, even those with direct geniculate input.

There is a large difference in the behaviour of orientation-specific cells. (True/False)

4. We find striking differences among orientation-specific cells, not just in optimum stimulus orientation or in the position of the receptive field on the retina, but in the way cells behave. The most useful distinction is between two classes of cells: *simple* and *complex*. As their names suggest, the two types differ in the complexity of their behavior, and we make the reasonable assumption that the cells with the simpler behavior are closer in the circuit to the input of the cortex.

Scientific American Library, 1988

Text C

The Genes for Colour Vision

Jeremy Nathans, 1989

Many research projects in psychophysics, physiology and chemistry have shown that our vision of colours is composed of three fundamental colours, Red, Green and Blue (an application of this principle being found in the colour television). Three types of cones (cells of the retina) are thus specialized according to the pigments they contain. Genetics has recently confirmed this research by isolating these three pigments and retracing their evolution from our common genetic ancestor, the monkey.

1. We therefore concluded that these genes encode the red and green pigments, and later studies we did with Piantanida confirmed this belief. The third gene, now known to encode the blue pigment, came from *chromosome* 7*, a finding that is consistent with the notion that variant blue color vision is determined by a nonsex chromosome.

2. The significant homology between the *rhodopsin** gene and the three *cone-pigment genes** suggested that all four genes had indeed evolved from the same *ancestor**. The available evidence supported the notion that at some early stage a primordial gene had given rise to three others: the rhodopsin gene, the blue-pigment gene and a third gene that encoded a pigment sensitive to light in the red-to-green part of visible *spectrum**. This third gene recently duplicated, yielding a red- and a green-pigment gene.

3. We think the red- and green-pigment genes are the product of fairly recent duplication, because they have a strikingly high degree of homology: a full 98 percent of their *DNA** is identical, suggesting it has had little time to change. The idea that the event took place not long ago, at least in evolutionary terms, is supported by the findings of Gerald H. Jacobs of the University of California at Santa Barbara, who worked with Bowmaker and Mollon. They have shown that New World (South American) monkeys have only a single visual-pigment gene on the *X-chromosome**. In contrast, Old World (African) monkeys, which are more closely related to human beings, appear to have two visual-pigment genes on that chromosome. The addition of the second X-chromosome gene must have occurred sometime after the separation of South America and Africa, and hence of the gene pools of the New and Old World monkeys, some 40 million years ago.

Scientific American, February 1989

Comprehension

a) Read the text carefully right through, then fill in the following chart:

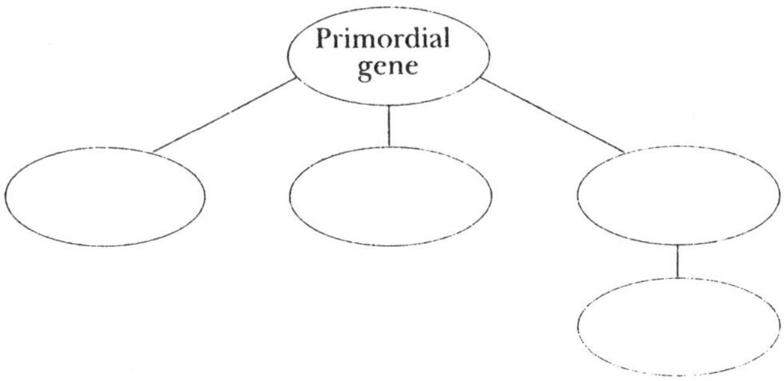

b) What evidence suggests that duplication of the red and green-pigmented gene took place fairly recently?

Text D

How to Make a Language User

Allan Collins and Ross Quillian, 1972

Collins and Quillian idealize Wiener's main objective and formulate a common science to study the machine and the brain. Ross Quillian is a computer scientist who wished to make a software package for simultaneous translation. He turned to the psychologist, Allan Collins to find out about the storage of word meaning in the memory. From their studies, original both in theory and method, one of the most significant fields of research was born—that of the semantic memory.

1. Concepts are represented by *lists** in computers because present day computers are serial processors. If parallel machines were built, then the necessity for ordering properties in a list would disappear. In fact, human concepts are probably more like *hooks or nodes** in a network from which many different properties hang.

2. So far, this just describes an association network of concepts which we think is a thoroughly plausible way to start building a computer memory to mimic human memory. Giuliano (1963) has indicated how such an association network could be represented in an analog computer. The trouble with a simple *association network** is that it does not specify the relation of properties to concepts. Worms are related to birds because birds eat them (though they are undoubtedly related in other ways too), and to dogs because worms live in a dog's coat of hair. The particular relation is as important to the property as the concepts that are related. Any memory structure that sloughs over these differences could never deal very intelligently with human language.

3. The relations between concepts are as varied as concepts themselves; indeed, relations are concepts and can be handled in many of the same ways as concepts that correspond to nouns or adjectives. Even adjective concepts such as red or square differ in their relation to different concepts they modify. For example, green is related to grass in a different way than yellow is to canary, since the green penetrates the grass and the yellow is only superficial to the canary. Both relations are different from the relation of blue to sky, since the blue is only in the atmosphere of earth during the day. These examples illustrate that relations can be quite complex, even though the question of "What color is grass?" can be answered without getting into these complexities. Any representation of relations in a computer must permit them to be as detailed as necessary; in other words, the description of a relation must be embeddable.

4. There is no reason why a semantic memory should consist only of a network of descriptive properties. Concepts are built up out of sensori-motor experience as well as language use, and there is every evidence that people utilize imagery extensively. (See, for example, Paivio, 1969; Bower, in press; Begg & Paivio, 1970.) In computers, the work of Gelernter (1963) and Baylor (1971) suggests that it would be helpful to project concepts on a display screen where they can be manipulated as geometric forms rather than property lists. This could be done within a semantic memory by an image generation routine which uses descriptive properties as *stored variables** for constructing a visual image. For a concept like canary, the color *attribute** would produce a light yellow color in the image, whereas, for bird, the lack of a specific color value would produce a color-vague image like those shown in a dictionary.

in *Organization of Memory*
Tulving and Donaldson,
Academic Press, 1972.

1. *Comprehension*

Read the text right through, then answer the following:

Para 1: What is the disadvantage of representing concepts as lists in a computer?
Para 2: Why is an association network approach insufficient?
Para 3: Why is the representation of relations between concepts so complex?
Para 4: The author suggests visual display to solve the problem. What do you think are the advantages and limitations of this?

2. *Vocabulary*

From the context of the text, try to guess at the meaning of the words below:

Hooks Nodes Network To slough over Embeddable

3. *Activity*

What is the "semantic" relationship of these colours to our culture and surroundings?

- black
- white
- purple

Text E

Some Effects of Grammatical Transformations on the Recall of English Sentences

Jacques Mehler, 1963

Computer science also influenced linguistic and researchers such as Chomsky developed a theory of language as a procedural formula. Language is not a conditioning by sounds (the controversy between Chomsky and Skinner is well-known) but composed of deep structures (the kernel sentence, subject and verbal syntagmatic) and the rules of transformation. These syntactic rules—generative or transformational grammar, analogous to the rules of the computer—allow us to generate any possible utterance. Linguistic psychologists were immediately attracted by this theory; it is richer than a simple interpretation in terms of conditioning.

1. The fact that a person can often rephrase "in his own words" the general sense of a message that he has not yet memorized in precise detail would seem to indicate that semantic components of a *meaningful** message are generally easier to recall than are its specific grammatical details. In the present experiment, therefore, we have attempted to explore this possible difference in a systematic manner. In general terms, the strategy adopted was the following: a set of eight short sentences was presented to the S, who was instructed that he would be tested for *recall**. The sentences differed systematically in their grammatical forms; they might be either active or passive, affirmative or negative, declarative or interrogative. The S's responses were then scored both for semantic accuracy (did he recall one of the eight sentences, regardless of grammatical form?) and for syntactic accuracy (given that a sentence was recalled, was its grammatical form correct?). The results of a preliminary study using this general approach have already been reported by Miller (1962).

2. The syntactic description used here is essentially Chomsky's (1957). According to Chomsky's grammar, most sentences are derived from more fundamental ones by certain special rules, called transformations. The fundamental, or kernel (*K*), sentences are, in the vocabulary of traditional grammar, simple, active, affirmative, declarative sentences, such as *The boy has hit the ball, The girl has worn the jewel,* etc. Only three grammatical transformations are considered in this experiment: the negative

(*N*), the passive (*P*), and the interrogative (*Q*). When the *N* transformation is applied to *The boy has hit the ball* it produces a new sentence, *The boy hasn't hit the ball.* When *P* is applied to the same *K* sentence, it produces *The ball has been hit by the boy.* The *Q* transformation applied to the same *K* sentence produces *Has the ball been hit by the boy?* These transformations may also be applied in combination to produce, for example, a passive-negative-question *(PNQ), Hasn't the ball been hit by the boy?*

Journal of Verbal Learning and Verbal Behavior,
1963, 2, 346-351.

Comprehension

a) Read the text quickly then answer the questions:

– We remember meanings, not words	True / False / Not stated
– Meaning was not tested	True / False / Not stated
– Grammar was tested	True / False / Not stated
– Miller supervised this text	True / False / Not stated
– Chomsky's theories are essential	True / False / Not stated

b) Now write a similar series of transformations for the sentences:

- The woman had worn the dress
- The children would have taken the test.

Text F

Personality and Assessment

Walter Mischel, 1968

With several other social psychologists, Mischel launched a critical study of the personality. The results of his research put the subjectivity of results into question and have started a new field of research into the personality.

Personality theory, experimental personality research, and *assessment** have quite different histories and their mutual implications have not been explored thoroughly. Courses on personality theory usually review the concepts advocated by different authors and offer omnibus surveys of psychological conceptions of man. Personality assessment, on the other hand, typically is relegated into the "how to do it" practical domain, and is inserted as an applied, independent course on assorted measurement techniques. Especially distressing, most approaches to personality still remain largely separated from developments in behavior theory and experimental research, in spite of many protests and some major efforts to the contrary (Bandura & Walters, 1963; Rotter, 1954).

Progress in the area of personality psychology and assessment has been hindered by the failure to apply relevant principles about the conditions that produce, maintain, and modify social behavior. The principles that emerge from *basic research** too often have not been seen as directly relevant to the understanding of the determinants of test responses in the clinic or the assessment project. It is as if we live in two independent worlds: the abstractions and artificial situations of the laboratory and the realities of life. In part this dualism between research and practice has resulted from the failure of basic psychological research to deal with social problems relevant to persons. Until fairly recently most experimental research offered as an aid in the understanding of human social behavior was not only nonsocial, in the sense of not dealing with interpersonal conditions, but also nonhuman, the subjects usually being rats, pigeons, or monkeys. Research with persons was confined largely to *correlational studies**, most frequently interrelating the *checking responses** of college students on different *paper-and-pencil inventories**. More recently, however, exciting progress has occurred in experimental social research with people. The resulting principles and techniques are being applied to the measurement and modification of the complex problems of persons—often severely disturbed persons.

Ed. J. Wiley and Sons, 1968.

1. *Vocabulary*

Give the best definitions of the following words :

- thoroughly
  - ❑ usefully
  - ❑ properly
  - ❑ badly
- omnibus
  - ❑ comprehensive
  - ❑ limited
  - ❑ non-stop
- distressing (in this context)
  - ❑ agonizing
  - ❑ unfortunate
  - ❑ unpleasant

- to hinder
  - ❑ to prevent
  - ❑ to help
  - ❑ to encourage
- relevant
  - ❑ useless
  - ❑ pleasant
  - ❑ meaningful

2. *Comprehension*

Now read the text to the end and answer the question which follow it.

– What is the difference between courses on personality theory and personality assessment?
– Are approaches to research in personality and behavior theory similar?
– What is inhibiting progress in the area of personality psychology?
– What has been the main failure of recent psychological research?
– Is this problem continuing?
– At the end of the text, why does the author sound optimistic for the future?

Lexique

Ancestor : ancêtre

L'ancêtre est un gène, le gène ancien qui, après évolution, a produit la rhodopsine et les gènes des pigments colorés.

Assessment : évaluation (dans le sens de mesure)

Association network : réseau associatif

Si l'on ne fait aucune hypothèse sur les relations qui "accrochent", les concepts (hiérarchie ou emboîtement) ont abouti à un simple réseau d'associations (hypothèse déjà faite par les behavioristes, d'où le nom de "néoconnexionnisme" pour se raccrocher à l'associationnisme des behavioristes sans avoir l'air d'en être un !)

Attribute : attribut

Dans ce domaine, attribut, propriété et trait sémantique sont synonymes et ne sont que des préférences d'auteurs.

Basic research : recherche de base

Le sens est plutôt celui de "recherche empirique" ou tournée vers les applications sans analyse fine des multiples déterminants de la situation : ce qui est visé par l'auteur c'est la réponse d'un individu dans un questionnaire, qui est analysé comme un fait brut alors que c'est un fait complexe.

Cell : cellule (Dans le texte B cellule nerveuse ou neurone).

Checking responses : réponses cochées (d'un questionnaire).

Chromosome 7

L'homme a 23 paires de chromosomes que l'on numérote du plus long (N° 1) au plus petit (N° 23).

Conditioned reinforcer : renforcement conditionné ou renforcement secondaire.

Conditioned response friends : littéralement "amis de la réponse conditionnée"

L'anglais permet une formule plus ramassée. Tolman vise évidemment ses collègues associationnistes de sorte qu'un équivalent français respectant l'humour pourrait être "l'amicale du conditionnement".

Cone-pigment genes : gènes des pigments des cônes

Il y a 3 cônes contenant chacun un pigment, bleu ou rouge ou vert.

Correlational studies : études corrélationnelles

Les corrélations sont ensuite utilisées dans l'analyse factorielle pour extraire les facteurs de la personnalité.

Cue stimuli : stimulus indice (on dirait plutôt stimulus discriminatif)

Stimulus ne s'accorde plus au pluriel.

Discrimination box (apparatus) : boîte à discrimination

Le labyrinthe simple comprend un seul carrefour avec une seule discrimination entre un couloir de droite et un couloir de gauche.

DNA : ADN

C'est-à-dire Acide DesoxyriboNucléique, constituant des chromosomes, un gène étant une séquence d'ADN. Les adjectifs étant en anglais placés avant le nom, les sigles sont inversés en français et en anglais (avec parfois des faux amis, ainsi le sigle anglais AIDS signifie SIDA).

Eye Movement : mouvement oculaire

Il existe plusieurs types de mouvements des yeux, mais ceux qui sont étudiés dans le texte 2 sont des mouvements coordonnés des deux yeux selon un itinéraire précis.

Feature : trait

Une figure complexe est analysée par petits fragments élémentaires appelés "traits" (vertical, horizontal, couleur...).

Feature ring

La théorie de Noton et Stark propose que les traits moteurs et sensoriels soient régulièrement assemblés dans un "anneau" (ring) terme plus poétique que le terme "programme" (informatique) qu'il sous-entend.

Fixation : fixation

Les mouvements oculaires (coordonnés) comprennent une saccade (saut) et une fixation (pause pendant laquelle se fait l'enregistrement de la scène par la rétine).

Hooks or nodes : crochets ou nœuds

L'ordinateur permet aussi d'emboîter des sous-ensembles (directories), le nom d'un sous-ensemble pouvant être représenté comme un nœud dans une hiérarchie ressemblant à un arbre : le nœud correspondant à un embranchement. Les attributs des concepts peuvent se représenter comme des éléments "accrochés" (hooks) à des nœuds.

Increase the chances that the organism will repeat that behavior

Augmente la probabilité (les chances) que l'organisme répète ce comportement. Petite phrase anodine qui est tout simplement la définition technique du renforcement.

Learning : apprentissage

L'apprentissage a un statut de concept théorique chez les behavioristes, dont Skinner est un grand représentant ; l'apprentissage est le résultat d'associations entre stimulus et réponses, établies par conditionnement.

Lists : listes (d'instructions ou commandes)

Un ordinateur actuel traite les programmes, instruction par instruction (sériellement) ; Collins et Quillian ont donc représenté le sens des mots par des listes de propriétés (ou attributs).

Locus of attention : lieu (ou champ) de l'attention

Une fixation ne se fait pas au hasard mais est guidée par un processus central de guidage qu'on appelle l'attention.

Maze : labyrinthe

Le labyrinthe a été la situation de choix pour étudier l'apprentissage. Tolman, expérimentaliste extrêmement inventif en a fabriqué plusieurs, labyrinthe à 3 couloirs, labyrinthe radial, double labyrinthe en forme de T...

Meaningful : avec sens (ou signification)

Il fallait spécifier ce qui semble maintenant un pléonasme qu'un message avait du sens car les behavioristes avaient une prédilection pour l'étude des syllabes sans signification (avec l'illusion d'étudier le niveau zéro de la langue).

Memory trace

Toute conception matérialiste de la mémoire implique une conservation de l'information dans le cerveau ; mais faute d'en savoir plus sur les mécanismes en cause, on utilise toujours le terme de "trace" qui date de l'Antiquité.

Overtrained : sur-entraîné

Après la phase d'apprentissage permettant que l'animal aille au but (du labyrinthe) sans erreur, on continue les essais pour que l'apprentissage soit résistant.

Paper-and-pencil inventories : inventaire (ou questionnaire) "papier-crayon"

Une des qualités d'un test est sa facilité d'emploi afin de le faire passer à des échantillons parfois importants. Le questionnaire papier-crayon est pratique et rapide d'où son utilisation intensive (tend à être remplacé par le téléphone dans les sondages d'opinion avec les mêmes défauts que critique Mischel puisque la réponse repose entièrement sur la sincérité et l'introspection de la personne contactée).

Recall : rappel

La technique utilisée pour tester les transformations est le rappel des phrases mémorisées ; une autre technique courante du domaine est l'utilisation des temps de réaction (reaction time).

Reinforcement : renforcement

C'est à Skinner que l'on doit le concept de renforcement et sa définition. Le renforcement inclut les renforcements primaires (innés : récompenses et punitions) et les renforcements secondaires (conditionnés).

Response : réponse

Mais il s'agit de la réponse du neurone, c'est-à-dire d'une réponse bioélectrique (texte B).

Rhodopsin : rhodopsine

La rhodopsine (ou pourpre rétinien) est le pigment des bâtonnets (autre cellule photoréceptrice avec les cônes) le plus répandu de la rétine.

Scan path : parcours (ou itinéraire ou voie) de balayage

C'est le parcours des fixations lors des mouvements oculaires.

Scanning : balayage

Terme cybernétique qui signifie un survol méthodique d'une cible et par extension en perception, un survol de la scène visuelle.

Shape : modelage

Skinner a montré que l'apprentissage était plus rapide s'il était progressif. Prenant l'analogie du sculpteur, cette technique est décrite comme un "modelage"; on dit aussi en franglais shaping. Cette conception a donné l'application importante de l'enseignement programmé (ou plus récemment de l'apprentissage "step by step", pas à pas).

Shocking : choc (électrique)

Dans beaucoup d'expériences, le choc électrique est faible et correspond à un stimulus tactile (picotement) mais ici, il s'agit d'un choc douloureux qui doit entraîner une réaction de fuite.

Sign-gestalt expectation : structure signe d'anticipation

Emprunter tel quel "gestalt" difficile à traduire serait du germano-franglais ; le terme de structure convient à la conception intégratrice de Tolman.

Signal : signal

Ou plus techniquement "stimulus" ; c'est ce stimulus qui, conditionné à la nourriture, va devenir le renforcement.

Simultaneously : simultanément

Pavlov, le découvreur du conditionnement avait montré que le conditionnement est le plus efficace lorsque les deux stimulus sont simultanés, ce que Skinner a retrouvé dans le conditionnement opérant entre un stimulus et une réponse.

Spectrum : spectre (gamme de rayons de la lumière, du violet au rouge).

Striate cortex : cortex strié

Le cortex strié est la partie occipitale du cortex et qui est le centre le plus développé de l'analyse des signaux visuels (perception et mémoire visuelle-imagée).

Stored variables : variables stockées

Les variables stockées sont diverses, mots, instructions...

Training techniques : techniques d'entraînement

De même, l'entraînement chez Skinner correspond à un pré-apprentissage progressif. (voir shape).

Trial and error situation : situation par essai et par erreur

En général le "par essai et par erreur" s'applique plutôt à l'apprentissage, une des lois qu'avait montrées Thorndike, le pionnier de l'apprentissage chez l'animal.

Visual field : champ visuel

Hubel et son prédécesseur Kuffler ont montré que certaines cellules de la rétine étaient spécialisées pour "voir" une toute petite partie du champ visuel. Le terme se réfère dans le texte au champ visuel d'une ou quelques cellules de la rétine ; ces informations vont être transmises à la cellule étudiée dans le cortex.

X chromosome : chromosome X

Une des 23 paires de chromosomes est complète chez la femme (XX) et incomplète chez l'homme (XY), ce sont donc les chromosomes sexuels qui déterminent les différences entre sexe. L'auteur montre dans la suite de l'article que les gènes du rouge et du vert sont au bout du chromosome X d'où certaines vicissitudes (perte ou duplication) qui produisent le daltonisme (perte de la vision colorée pour le rouge, le vert ou ces deux couleurs).

Part 3

Differential Psychology

1

Measuring Intelligence

Lewis Terman and Maud Merrill, 1937

The psychometric scale of Alfred Binet and Théodore Simon was extremely successful in the USA and was adapted by Lewis Terman, professor at Stanford University, with the collaboration of Maud Merrill, an associate professor. This adaptation (called the "Stanford-Binet") was a much improved version. In France this version was further adapted and renamed the "Terman-Merrill". In this text the authors describe the principles that guided their adaptation of what was to become the first intelligence test.

(Do exercise 1 before reading the text)

1. The major faults of the original Stanford-Binet *scale** have long been recognized. Although affording a satisfactorily *valid** and *reliable** measure over a fairly wide intermediate range, it was especially defective at both extremes. Abilities below the mental level of four years or above that of the *average** adult were very inadequately sampled. In the range from five to ten years the *standardization** was surprisingly correct, considering the rather small number of subjects on which it was based, but above ten it yielded scores that were progressively too low. A number of tests in the scale were unsatisfactory because of low validity, difficulty of scoring, susceptibility to *coaching**, etc. The instructions both for administration and scoring in numerous instances lacked the precision which is necessary to insure objectivity and comparability of results. Finally, one of the severest limitations to the usefulness of the scale was the fact that no alternative form was available for use in retesting or as a safeguard against coaching.

The contents of Forms L and M are similar to the original scale. (True / False)

Form L is more accurately standardized than Form M. (True / False)

2. In the revision here offered we have provided two scales which differ almost completely in content, but are mutually equivalent with respect to difficulty, range, reliability, and validity. The scales are designated as Form L and Form M. In content Form L bears greater resemblance to the original Stanford-Binet, but neither form can be recommended above the other. Both, we believe, are relatively free from the grosser faults of the old scale. They cover a far wider range, they are more accurately standardized throughout, the tests provide a richer *sampling of abilities**, and the procedures have been more rigidly defined. On the whole they are somewhat less verbal than the old scale, especially in the lower years.

The revision utilizes the assumptions, methods, and principles of the age scale as conceived by Binet. There are of course other systems of tests which are meritorious, but for the all-round clinical appraisal of a subject's intellectual level the Binet type of scale has no serious rival.

Why did the authors use the same principles of the age scale as Binet?

How have the authors accounted for the cultural evolution of their younger subjects?

Why was it difficult to devise non-verbal tests for the upper levels?

What do the authors mean by "the level at which this shorthand functions?"

3. For the younger subjects the scale has been made incomparably more interesting and also more valid by the liberal use of diminutive objects, brightly colored cubes, wooden beads, and other attractive materials. In general, however, the content of the new scales resembles that of the old and includes such well-known test as comprehension, absurdities, word-naming, drawing designs, memory for digits, giving differences and similarities, defining abstract terms, etc.

4. Our efforts to increase the number of non-verbal tests were successful chiefly at the lower levels. Like other investigators we have found that is extremely difficult to devise non-verbal tests for the upper levels which satisfy the requirements of validity, reliability, and time economy. At these levels the major intellectual differences between subjects reduce largely to differences in the ability to do conceptual thinking, and facility in dealing with concepts is most readily sampled by the use of verbal tests. Language, essentially, is the short-hand of the higher thought processes, and the level at which this short-hand functions is one of the most important determinants of the level of the processes themselves.

How was subjective scoring discouraged?

Certain test items were rejected as they would have been difficult to score. (True/False)

5. One of the important aims of the revision was to secure greater objectivity of scoring. Where judgment is involved in evaluating responses to an item, definite principles and classified illustrations have been given to guide the examiner. Ease and objectivity of scoring have in fact often played a crucial rôle in the selection and rejection of test items. The part played by subjective judgment cannot be wholly eliminated from a test of the Binet type, but we have tried to bring it as near as possible to the irreductible minimum.

Selection of subjects for the tests was not so important as the selection of the tests themselves. (True/False)

The authors claim equivalence between Forms L and M of the test. How did they achieve this?

6. Hardly less important than the selection of suitable tests has been the selection of subjects for use in the standardization of the scales. We have devoted more than ordinary effort to secure a representative sampling of the white child population in the United States between the ages of two and eighteen years. Besides increasing the number of subjects tested to 100 at each half-year level below six, to 200 at each age between six and fourteen, and to 100 at each age from fifteen to eighteen, we have made a stubborn attempt to avoid sampling errors inherent in age, grade location, nationality, and geographical distribution. We do not flatter ourselves that we have been entirely successful, but our data represent a much closer approximation to an unbiased sampling than has heretofore been attained in the standardization of any scale for individual examining. The fact that the same subjects were used in the standardization of Form L and Form M has made it possible to guarantee almost perfect equivalence of the scores yielded by the two scales.

George G. Harrap & Company ltd.
London, Bombay, Sydney, 1937

Exercises 1

1. *Pre-reading activity*

Brainstorm: what criteria are necessary to make an effective intelligence test?

2. *Comprehension*

a) Paragraph 1 of this text is critical of the original Stanford-Binet scale. Read it quickly, noting what the authors say about:

- its measuring of the intermediate range
- its sampling of the extremes
- standardization in the 5-10 year age band
- certain tests in the scale
- administration considerations
- alternative forms.

b) Now compare your notes to the criteria in the pre-reading activity. After reading paragraph 1 of the text, can you add any criteria that you hadn't thought of earlier?

3. *Vocabulary*

Find words in the text which mean:

Para 1: to train
Para 1: to provide (information)
Para 1: to be insufficient
Para 3: small round objects
Para 4: mainly
Para 6: tenacious, persevering
Para 6: until now.

4. *Grammar review*

• **Comparison of adjectives.** You probably have little difficulty with the basic comparisons, such as:

James is older than Susan, but
Susan is more intelligent than James.

But why don't we say "intelligenter than" or "more old than"?

Look at the following table of costs for tests in three separate testing centres: A, B and C.

A	B	C
FF 1200	FF 1000	FF 600

Using the adjectives "dear", "expensive" and "cheap", what can we say?

– Fill in the blanks in the sentences below:

Tests in A are _______ _______ in B
Tests in A are _______ _______ _______ in B
Tests in B and C are _______ _______ in A
Tests in B and C are _______ _______ in A

– Also, in the case of the two extremes (A and C) what can we say? Use "- est", "the most", "the least" with the same adjectives:

A is _______ _______
A is _______ _______ _______
C is _______ _______
C is _______ _______ _______

Note that we can also say:

Tests in B are nearly as high as in A
Tests in C are not as high as in A or B
Tests in C are not so high as in A or B

(However, "so high as" – the affirmative, is incorrect).

- **Intensifiers and softeners**

As well as simply making comparisons between different elements, we often need to make these comparisons more precise. Look at the following chart:

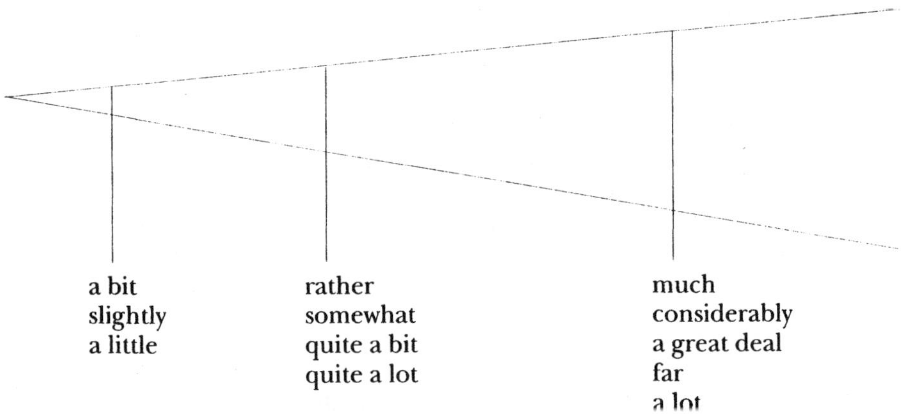

Thus we can say (for example):

Tests in A are slightly more expensive than in B, while those in C are by far the lowest..., etc.

These intensifiers and softeners are the classic ones, but there are many others.

– Now read paragraph 2 of the text, underlining the phrases of comparison as well as any expressions which intensify or soften these comparisons.

5. *Between the lines*

a) Look at the first sentence of paragraph 6:

"Hardly less important than the selection of suitable tests has been the selection of subjects for use in the standardization of the scales."
The rather elevated tone of this sentence is emphasized by its structure.
– Translate this sentence.
– Now re-formulate it, keeping the original meaning but making it more neutral.
Another example of this type of sentence is:
Hardly more important than the health service is the state of the nation's schools.

b) "Hardly" (as well as "scarcely" or "seldom") are difficult words when used to provide emphasis.

Translate the following:
– Hardly had he left university before he got married
– Seldom have I met such an idiot
– Scarcely had she arrived when a telegram called her away
– Seldom will we see his like again
– Never have I known such happiness
Note: the subject/auxiliary verb inversion.

6. *Translate into English*

Les tests ne sont pas toujours bien perçus dans le grand public sans doute pour différentes raisons, manque de confiance, risque d'erreur, transfert de son pouvoir à un autre (le psychologue), refus de mesurer l'esprit... Sur le principe un test est cependant justifié et il faut rappeler un peu d'histoire. Lorsque Alfred Binet construisit avec Théodore Simon le premier test d'intelligence, l'estimation de l'intelligence se faisait selon des critères subjectifs, largement basés sur des préjugés ancestraux : ainsi les enfants qui se rongeaient les ongles, les onychophages, étaient vus comme débiles. Un test est donc avant tout un instrument objectif de mesure : basé sur des épreuves qui peuvent être appliquées de la même façon et notées de la même façon par différents correcteurs, par exemple, une épreuve de vocabulaire consistera à définir des mots, une épreuve visuo-spatiale consistera à faire copier des figures géométriques, une épreuve de raisonnement numérique à résoudre des problèmes arithmétiques, etc. En deuxième lieu, un test doit être standardisé, c'est-à-dire soumis à un échantillon important de façon à comparer des résultats d'un sujet donné aux résultats de l'échantillon. On dira qu'un enfant a un développement normal si les résultats correspondent à la moyenne des résultats. Un test est donc un instrument objectif et statistique.
Beaucoup de soi-disant tests ne satisfont pas à ces critères et malheureusement, beaucoup de gens qui sont méfiants à l'égard des tests se jettent les yeux fermés dans des pratiques sans fondement scientifique, comme l'astrologie, la numérologie qui sont des croyances remontant aux

origines de la civilisation (les signes du zodiaque ont été découverts par les Babyloniens).
A l'inverse, il ne faut pas accorder une confiance aveugle dans les tests qui ne sont que des instruments. Les tests peuvent contenir des erreurs de construction, de standardisation, des personnes non expérimentées peuvent commettre des erreurs de passation (oublier de chronométrer une épreuve, oublier de s'assurer de la compréhension de la consigne...) et comme tout instrument, en physique par exemple, les tests sont des instruments perfectibles en fonction du développement scientifique et du développement culturel.

7. *Activity*

Astrology as a predictive test.
Collect and compare a number of astrological articles from different popular British newspapers and magazines. Do they predict the same things? Is there any underlying similarity of theme for the various signs of the zodiac?

2

The Measurement of Abilities

Philip E. Vernon, 1965

Following the research of Spearman, inventor of factorial analysis and of the general factor of intelligence, Vernon developed this theory further by breaking down the general factor into group factors. He carried out much research into the verbal-educative and mechanical-spatial factors among schoolchildren.

(Do question 1 before reading the text)

Until recently, psychological conceptions of ability have remained untested. (True/False)

What did the "faculty" school of psychologists do to train children's minds?

Why were they unsuccessful?

How does the present-day approach differ?

1. *Fallacious Views of Mental Organization.*—Correlational investigations have assumed especial importance in recent years, since they enable us to clarify our conceptions of human abilities, and of the organization or structure of the mind. The layman's notions as to what abilities exist, and what each ability includes or excludes, are extremely loose, and the same was true of psychological theory throughout most of last century. Teachers and parents are heard to remark: "Johnny is poor at book-learning, but he makes up for it by his cleverness with his hands. He will be a good mechanic when he grows up." "Mary has an excellent memory and good power of attention." "Willie is slow but sure," and so on. Such statements are now known, as a result of experimental investigation, to be largely fallacious. Only exact study can tell us how far the slow person is likely to be sure, whether manual ability in a boy has any predictive value for mechanical ability in a man, whether there is any such entity in the mind as memory. Again, the so-called faculty school of psychologists of a hundred years ago considered the mind to be made up of a number of distinct powers or faculties such as reasoning, judgment, imagination, etc. Indeed, it was at one time regarded as the main object of education to train each of these faculties by providing children with appropriate 'mental gymnastics.' As soon, however, as scientific psychologists tried to define the faculties precisely and measure them, and to determine the effects upon them of various types of training, they fell into discredit. *A priori* analysis has not even been able to decide what is the true nature of intelligence. The accounts of it given by different writers have been extremely varied and discrepant. Nowadays, therefore, such problems, both of theory and practice, are approached by means of experimental studies of correlations between tests. For they all eventually resolve into the question—what correlates with what?

Define "low correlation" performances.

Think of an example of a "specific" performance.

What three criteria are necessary for mechanical ability to be recognized as an entity?

In the author's view, can mechanical ability be tested?

2. *The Scientific Definition of an* Ability*.—First we must define what we mean by an ability, capacity, or faculty. It implies the existence of a group or category of performances which correlate highly with one another, and which are relatively distinct from (i.e. give low correlations with) other performances. Take, for example, mechanical ability. Some people are better than others at tasks involving manipulations of mechanisms, and this ability is fairly *consistent* or *general* in the sense that those who are good at one such task are also usually good at others. The *consistency** is not perfect. A may be especially good with meccano, less clever with locks, B the opposite, C the best with electrical fittings, and so on. But if there was no appreciable correlation between these and other similar performances; if they were all found to be *specific,* we should not be entitled to regard mechanical ability as a real entity. Another important condition is that the performances should be fairly reliable. We do not expect perfect stability, but if people fluctuated wildly in their success at mechanical tasks from day to day, we should hardly recognize the existence of mechanical ability. There is a further possibility, namely, that the various performances may intercorrelate well, but that the correlations may be accounted for by some other common factor such as *general intelligence** (the age factor, we will assume, has already been eliminated). Mechanical ability would not then be anything distinctive. However, intelligence tests can be applied to the same persons who take the mechanical tests, and intelligence can be *partialed out** or held constant. It is then found that the mechanical tests still overlap, or show positive correlations with one another over and above their correlations due to the intelligence factor. We are, therefore, able to accept mechanical ability as something consistent and distinctive. Tests of it do correlate sufficiently well and reliably for us to postulate some common element running through them.

What is the difference between a "group" factor and a "general" factor?

3. A common element such as this is often referred to as a *group factor**, since it occurs in a group of performances of a certain restricted type. It differs from a *general factor* like intelligence, which is found to run through an extremely wide range of tests, which indeed enters to some extent into all abilities.

A single group factor test is sufficient. (True/False)

How is arithmetical ability measured?

4. Since the consistency or overlapping of different mechanical tests is not perfect, no one test can give a really adequate measurement of mechanical ability. But by combining several tests we are likely to get a result much more representative of the group factor as a whole. The same applies, of course, in the measurement of educational abilities. We do not expect long-division sums alone to tell us how good pupils are at arithmetic, although they provide some indication of the ability. Instead we set several types of sums, and try to cover the whole field of arithmetic which the pupils are supposed to know.

Memory-testing is a waste of time. (True/False)

5. Arithmetic is likely to yield a group factor similar to the mechanical ability factor. But many of the faculties assumed by psychologists in the past, or by laymen at the present time, fail to

What does the author imply in admitting the existence of "small group factors" of memory?

stand up to the criteria enumerated above. Memory, for example, refers to so many different things, that it is meaningless to talk of so-and-so as having a good or bad memory in general, or of 'training children's memories.' The speeds with which people learn various sorts of material, and their retentiveness (i.e. the amounts of such material which they can recall after an interval), give only moderate or low inter-correlations, especially when the influence of intelligence is removed. Probably there exist several small group factors, each representing memory for a certain narrow range of material. In other words, there may be several types, but no single entity, of memory.

Mental speed is opposed to mental accuracy. (True/False)

"He's slow and unsure". How was this demonstrated?

6. The notion that mental speed differs from, and is usually opposed to, mental accuracy or power also appears to be fallacious. If there were two quite distinct abilities, then tests of speed should give high correlations with one another, and low or negative correlations with tests of accuracy or power. Under appropriate conditions of testing, difficult untimed tests and easy speeded tests do yield somewhat different results; thus a partial distinction is indicated. But they still correlate positively to a moderate or a high degree, showing that, on the whole, those who are 'slow' at mental work are more likely to be 'unsure' than 'sure.'

Tests of manual abilities do not correlate with those of mental abilities. (True/False)

Why do you think groups of university students occasionally show negative correlations?

7. *All Mental Abilities are Positively Inter-correlated.*—Let us now turn to the wider problem—what abilities does the mind contain, and how are they organized or inter-related? A first, extremely important, fact is that all tests of mental abilities tend to give positive inter-correlations. Even tests of manual, physical, and other non-intellectual functions also usually correlate positively with one another and with mental tests, though the coefficients are often very small, whereas the coefficients among tests of intellectual functions are generally moderate to high. In selected groups, such as university students, occasional negative correlations may arise; but these are not typical, and they are seldom statistically significant.

University of London Press, 1965
St Paul's House, Warwick Lane, London EC4
pp. 130-132

Exercises 1

1. *Pre-reading activity*

Two of the key words in the text are:
– ability – intelligence.

a) Ability: other words notionally linked to "ability" are:

Capacity Skill Talent

Place them in the following sentences:
- She's a promising singer and has a lot of _______ .
- She has the _______ to do better at school if only she worked harder.
- Repairing clocks is a difficult _______ to master.

b) Intelligence: words linked to the adjective "intelligent" are:

Wise Bright Clever

- The old man didn't go to school but he's very _______ .
- She's very _______ with her hands.
- He's very _______ and should make a good salesman.

2. *Comprehension check*

a) Read the first paragraph (lines 7-16 only) and quickly note down why:
- Johnny may not be a good mechanic
- Mary's "power of attention" is questionable
- Willy may grow up to be slow and careless.

b) Now read the second paragraph (lines 9-11 only) and say if these statements are true:
- B may be clever with locks
- A may be better at meccano than B and C
- C may be less clever than B with electrical fittings.

3. *Vocabulary*

Match these words with their definitions:

A layman — 1 during
B throughout — 2 denominated
C so-called — 3 non-specialist
D discrepant — 4 extend too far
E overlap — 5 varied

A	B	C	D	E

4. *Grammar review*

- **The present tense**

Much of this text is written in the present simple tense. This is logical enough in a text dealing with current (i.e. 1965) states, attitudes and opinions.
(* It is standard publication practice for the preterite to be used to describe experiments and methodology which were completed at the time the article was written while results and theoretical principles are

described in the present tense, as they are assumed to possess a general validity).
We will look briefly at how emphasis is achieved, then deal with some other circumstances where the present tense is used.

- **Emphasis**

Look at this sentence:

Tests of mechanical ability correlate well

Now look at the last sentence in paragraph 2:

"Tests of (mechanical ability) do correlate sufficiently well..."

The use of the "dummy auxiliary" in an affirmative sentence serves to emphasize "correlate".

– *"Strengthen" the following present and past sentences in a similar manner:*

The orchestra played wonderfully, didn't it?
She looks beautiful this evening
They worked hard to pass the exam
He smokes thirty cigarettes a day, you know
I believe you

- **Other uses of the present simple**

a) They play chess every Saturday morning (a "habit") compared to:
They are playing chess (an action taking place or planned for the near future).

b) He lives in London (a permanent fact) compared to: He is living in London at the moment (implying a temporary state).

c) The plane takes off at 5 o'clock (future time, as fact).

– *Put the most appropriate form of the present (emphatic, simple or progressive) into the following sentences:*

I _______ (to live) in Paris at the moment but I'll move to Grenoble next year.
"I wish you'd believe me. I _______ (to love) you", he shouted desperately.
She _______ (to use) my car to go to work this week, but normally she _______ (to go) by train.
We _______ (to go) to the country tomorrow.
I _______ (to want) him to go to university, but he _______ (to insist) on leaving school when he's 16.

5. *Between the lines*

At certain places in the text, the author, in his doubtless meritorious desire to elucidate his ideas with exactitude, tends to be a little ponderous (rather like this sentence). The structure of such sentences should not pose a great problem as they are fairly close to French constructions. But following the author's thought processes is not always easy.

Look at this sentence from paragraph 1:
"As soon, however, as scientific psychologists tried to define the faculties precisely and measure them, and to determine the effects upon them of various types of training, they fell into discredit." Although a little ponderous, this is not a badly-written sentence. It is almost impossible to simplify while keeping the meaning intact.
However, the following sentences are deliberately badly-written.

Re-formulate and simplify them without leaving out essentials:

a) However hard he tried, and it can be stated with certainty that he tried very hard for he was naturally stubborn, Tom did not succeed in gaining the respect ot the other boys in the class, who continued to hate him.

b) Although it must be readily understood by all citizens that in times of national crisis such as this, the state will in no way infringe upon human rights, a small number of special laws will be passed with the aim of temporarily limiting public criticism of the government.

6. *Text content*

Using the following notes and appropriate link notions as indicated, write a summary of paragraph 1. (Do not refer to the text during this exercise).

Correlational investigations important recently
Cause
structure of mind can be clarified
Layman's present notions of ability
Similarity
psychological theory of 19th century
Different abilities can only be measured after study
Addition
19th century psychologists considered mind as
"parcelled out" abilities *Addition*
Parcelling out led to "mental gymnastics" training
Contrast
Psychologists found it impossible to define abilities
Effect
nowadays problems approached by experimental studies.

7. *Activity*

Paragraph 5 : Memory.
Early tests started by taking a sample of scholastic activities as being representative of intelligence. Imagine and describe – in English – the elements that could make up a memory test (such as, memories of daily life, of things learned at school or of leisure activities...).

Text A

The Louisville Twin Study

Ronald Wilson, 1983

To demonstrate the role of genetics in behavior, research into twins was chosen by this team from the University of Louisville, which specialized in these studies conducted over three generations of researchers (from Falkner in 1957, then Vandenberg and finally Wilson, the author of this text). In this remarkable scientific "relay race" approximately 500 pairs of twins were studied, from birth to 15 years old.

Why are infant twins of interest in studying behavioral development?

1. A longitudinal research program with infant twins offers a powerful resource to study the determinants of behavioral development. Monozygotic *(MZ)** twins provide the rare natural experiment with humans in which two zygotes share exactly the same genotype and are raised in the same family environment.

Do dizygotic twins differ genetically from other siblings?

Do they differ in any other way?

How can we estimate genetic and other influences on these groups of children?

2. Dizygotic *(DZ)** twins, by contrast, share a variable number of genes in common (50 % on the average), proportionally the same as any other pair of *siblings** from the same family. However, dizygotic twins have further shared the homogeneous experiences of being born and raised as twins, which should enhance their similarity in comparison to siblings. If the collective influences of gene action and *prenatal and postnatal** environment dictate the course of mental development, then the contributions of the various factors may be estimated from comparison of monozygotic twins with dizygotic twins and nontwin siblings.

3. The Louisville Twin Study was initiated more than 25 years ago (Falkner, 1957), and the backbone of the program is the large number of young twins who have made regular visits to the study for testing. At present, there are 494 pairs of twins active in the longitudinal study, ranging in age from 3 months to 15 years. Recruitment has been an ongoing process, with 25-35 pairs added each year since 1963.

How was the sample made representative?

How did the resaerchers cope with frequently-moving families?

4. The twins have been recruited from the Board of Health records of twin births in the metropolitan Louisville area, and a special effort has been made to make the sample as representative as possible. In terms of socio-economic status, 27 % of the twin families are *ranked** in the lowest two *deciles** of the occupational *rating scale** (Reiss, 1961); 11 % are in the highest two deciles. The other families are distributed in roughly equal proportions among the six intermediate deciles (8.8 %-11.8 %). Attrition has been minimal because of intensive efforts to follow up on families that move frequently and to maintain their cooperation.

5. *Zygosity determination.— Zygosity** was established for same-sex pairs by *blood typing** on 22 or more red cell antigens (Wilson, 1980). If the results were concordant for all antiserum tests, the twins were classified as monozygotic; if the results were discordant for any test, dizygotic. For technical reasons, the blood typing was deferred until the twins were 3 years old, so the infant tests were completed before zygosity was established. Opposite-sex twins were classified as dizygotic on the basis of the sex difference.

Child Development, 1983, 54, 298-316.

1. *Vocabulary check*

Guess the meaning of the following words from their contexts:

Para 1: to be raised
Para 2: further
Para 2: to enhance
Para 3: backbone
Para 4: records
Para 4: attrition

2. *Statistics*

Are the following statements probably true or false? Check in paragraph 3.

Out of 100 pairs of twins:

- fewer than a quarter came from working class families
- about ten came from professional families
- a large proportion came from rich environments
- the majority came from upper-middle or middle class environments
- the poor were badly represented

Text B

Tests as Instruments of Research

Ronald Wilson, 1983

Tests are too often considered as simply diagnostic instruments in child evaluation. The use of tests as an objective measure and comparison in research has long been underestimated. One of the essential requirements of follow-up tests such as those in Louisville is a good level of standardization to ensure a valid comparison at different ages.

(Do exercise 1 before reading the text)

Twins will be tested at nine months of age. (True/False)
Twins will be tested once during their third year. (True/False)
Twins will not be tested at ten years of age. (True/False)
Why were new tests integrated into the program?

1. *Ages at testing.*—The *twins** are tested initially at 3 months of age, and they make subsequent visits every 3 months during the first year, every 6 months during the second and third years, and annually thereafter to age 9 years. A final *follow-up** test is scheduled at age 15 years. The ongoing nature of recruitment means that many twins have not completed 15 full years in the program, but nearly two-thirds of the sample have test data covering at least 6 consecutive years.

2. *Tests of mental development.*—The tests employed in this program have been selected from the best *standardized** and most carefully constructed *psychometric** tests available. In this regard, some new and revised tests for preschool children have become available within the past 15 years which represent major advances in assessment. Bayley's life-time work in mental development culminated in the Bayley Scales of Infant Development (1969), and it was the first well-standardized instrument for infant appraisal. The *Stanford-Binet** Form L-M was restandardized on a fresh sample in 1972 (Terman & Merrill, 1973), and these new norms corrected for many of the deficiencies in the original 1937 standardization sample.

How did McCarthy's scales differ from the WPPSI?
What was the advantage of the WISCR over its predecessor?

3. The Wechsler Preschool and Primary Scale of Intelligence (*WPPSI**) was published in 1967 (Wechsler, 1967), and it represented a well-standardized downward extension of the Wechsler Intelligence Scale for Children. The McCarthy Scales of Children's Abilities (McCarthy, 1972) were recently published, and while the scales differed somewhat in focus from the Binet and WPPSI—particularly by avoiding any reference to IQ—nevertheless they sampled domains of cognitive abilities that were collectively metricized by a general cognitive index. Finally, the revised version of the Wechsler Intelligence Scale for Children (WISC-R) was released in 1974, and it updated the norms, items, and scoring of the WISC to contemporary standards (Wechsler, 1974).

What makes these tests unique?

4. The importance of such standardized psychometric instruments can hardly be over-estimated. They furnish a means of appraising mental development during a period of rapid growth, as well as a means of obtaining a *reliable** assessment of individual differences. Children are compared with a representative sample of their age peers, and their relative placement (whether advanced or delayed) is expressed in a *standard-score** format that remains constant across ages and tests. Episodes of acceleration and lag now become interpretable as genuine phenomena, not simply as *by-products** of measurement error.

5. These crucial features of standardization and scoring have never been available in previous tests, and in a literal sense the recent tests may be classified as benchmarks of mental measurement. When employed with a longitudinal twin sample from birth into the school years, the tests yield a detailed picture of each twin's mental development from infancy onward and a measure of concordance among *co-twins**.

6. *Tests and ages.*—The Bayley Mental Scale has been administered at 3, 6, 9, 12, 18 and 24 months of age; the Stanford-Binet at 30 and 36 months; the WPPSI at 4, 5, and 6 years; and the WISC or WISC-R at 7, 8, 9, and 15 years. Recently the McCarthy test has been substituted for the WPPSI at 4 years because it gives a broader sample of the child's behavior at this age. Each test converts the *raw scores** into *age-adjusted standard scores** with a mean of 100 and SD of 16 (15 for the WPPSI and WISC).

How many examiners saw each twin during the test period?

7. At each visit, the twins were tested by separate examiners, who also alternated between the twins over successive visits. The test procedures were rehearsed intensively to assure comparability among examiners, and the test scoring was verified by a third examiner before the scores were recorded.

Child Development, 1983, 54, 298-316.

1. *Vocabulary check*

Connect these words with their meanings:

A Thereafter	1 milestone
B ongoing	2 estimate
C appraisal	3 from that moment
D lag	4 wide
E benchmark	5 retardation
F broad	6 wide

A	B	C	D	E	F

2. *Text content*

With reference to paragraph 6, look at this chart and point out any inaccuracies:

Test periodicity	*Test*
every three months	Bayley Mental Scale
used twice	Stanford-Binet
used three times	WPPSI
annually until 19 years old	WISC
at 4 years old	WPPSI

Lexique

Ability : aptitude ou facteur

Dans ces conceptions, l'intelligence est multiple et considérée comme regroupant plusieurs mécanismes différents regroupés sous le terme d'aptitude.

Age-ajusted standard scores : scores standardisés ajustés par âge

La distribution des scores bruts ne donne évidemment pas (sauf coïncidence) la même moyenne ni le même écart-type de sorte que les distributions ne sont pas comparables à des âges différents. On égalise donc par un procédé statistique (standardisation) les distributions en transformant les notes de façon à ce que la moyenne et l'écart-type soit le même ; dans le domaine des tests, on prend par convention une moyenne de QI de 100 et un écart-type de 16 (écart-type fréquent) sauf pour les tests de Wechsler (l'inventeur de la standardisation des QI) qui sont déjà standardisés avec un écart-type de 15.

Average : moyenne (au sens statistique du terme)

Blood typing : groupes sanguins (tests biologiques qui assurent que les jumeaux ont les mêmes gènes (MZ) ou non (DZ)

By-product : erreur de mesure ; arte-fact.

Coaching : exercice, entraînement

Un entraînement peut survenir lorsque le test est passé plusieurs fois ; c'est pour pallier cet inconvénient que Terman et Merrill ont construit une deuxième version "parallèle" du test primitif.

Consistency : consistance

Plutôt traduit par le terme de "fidélité" en psychométrie pour indiquer qu'une épreuve mesure la même aptitude à des moments différents ou par "homogénéité" pour indiquer que les items d'une épreuve mesurent la même aptitude.

Co-twins : co-jumeaux

Jumeaux vrais ou faux mais d'une même paire, c'est-à-dire d'une même famille.

Decile : décile

Division en dixième d'une distribution, ici des niveaux socio-économiques (occupational scale).

DZ : DZ ; jumeaux Di-Zigotes
C'est-à-dire issus de deux œufs différents (deux ovules différents fécondés par deux spermatozoïdes différents) autrement dit des faux jumeaux.

Follow-up : littéralement "suivi"
Techniquement étude longitudinale : c'est-à-dire suivi des mêmes individus (ici des enfants) sur une longue période ; contrairement à l'étude transversale (cross-sectional study) qui étudie des "tranches d'âge" au même moment donc des individus différents.

General intelligence : intelligence générale
Représente le facteur général de Spearman ou chez Vernon, qui est beaucoup plus prudent sur le plan théorique, un facteur commun.

Group factor : facteur de groupe (cf. contexte)

MZ : MZ ; jumeaux Mono-Zygotes
C'est-à-dire issus d'un même œuf (zygote en biologie) : vrais jumeaux.

Partialed out : neutralisé
Certaines analyses peuvent neutraliser une variable, l'âge par exemple, pour mettre en évidence l'effet d'une autre variable.

Prenatal and postnatal : prenatal et postnatal
Prenatal concerne les influences avant la naissance, intra-utérines, rencontrées par le fœtus dans le ventre de sa mère ; la ressemblance des faux jumeaux dans les premiers mois montre l'importance des influences prénatales.

Psychometric : psychométrique
Mesure psychologique par des instruments objectifs (tests).

Ranked : rangés, ordonnés

Rating scale : échelle de mesure

Raw scores : scores bruts
Ce sont les résultats aux épreuves avant standardisation.

Reliable : littéralement "sûr" ; plutôt "fidèle" en psychométrie c'est-à-dire qui donne les mêmes mesures à différents moments de test.

Sampling of abilities : échantillonnage d'aptitudes
Le Binet-Simon est le premier d'une longue dynastie de tests qu'on peut appeler "composite" car ils correspondent à un "échantillonnage" d'épreuves variées correspondant aux diverses

activités intellectuelles de la vie quotidienne, en particulier de la vie scolaire. Ce type de test ne repose pas sur une définition de l'intelligence mais est un instrument empirique, basé sur l'expérience et le tâtonnement.

Scale : échelle

L'épreuve de Binet est construite à partir d'épreuves (items en franglais) caractéristique d'un âge moyen, formant autant "d'échelons" gradués comme dans une échelle. C'est aux États-Unis que l'échelle d'intelligence a pris le nom de "test", mot importé par la suite en France.

Siblings : frères et sœurs

Au sens large, c'est-à-dire selon les familles, deux frères, deux sœurs ou un frère et une sœur : le terme américain est très économique.

Standard-score : score standardisé

Standardization : standardisation

Mesure des scores sur un groupe de référence

Standardized : standardisé

Sous-entendu sur le plan statistique

Stanford-Binet

Version américaine du test Binet-Simon par Terman et Merrill à l'université de Stanford d'où son nom de "Terman-Merrill" en France.

Twins : jumeaux

Valid : valide

WPPSI : adaptation du test de Wechsler pour les enfants d'âge préscolaire.

Zygosity : gémellité (type de jumeau, vrai ou faux)

Part 4

Child Psychology and Education

1

The Origin of Language

Orvis C. Irwin, 1949

How have humans, once adult, managed to acquire a vocabulary of some tens of thousand words? This question has always fascinated psychologists. Since this classic study, research has been centred around the role of dialogue in its cultural context with parents or with other children at nursery school.

(Do exercise 1 before reading the text)

1. A question frequently asked about our investigation is, "Where do you get your babies?" Obviously this is the simplest aspect of the whole endeavor, for there are plenty of babies in the world. However, the question does lead directly to the general problem of sampling the population of babies. One good source of subjects is a nursery connected with the obstetrical department of a hospital, and a great deal of our work has been done in this situation.

2. The home is another natural laboratory for this work. After a baby is taken home from the hospital, it is visited at regular intervals of two weeks or a month throughout infancy. At each visit a sample of the baby's speech, as uttered on a number of breaths, is written down in the International Alphabet. If care is taken to select homes of different socio-economic status, the speech sound samples may reflect a number of variables operating in the home situation, and the data subsequently may be analyzed in terms of these variables.

3. We have studied infants' speech development in several other situations: in orphanages, where retardation in speech is notoriously frequent; in state institutions for the feeble-minded; in schools for the deaf, where the investigation of how children deaf from birth achieve intelligible speech makes a valuable comparison with the development of speech in the normal infant.

How many basic sounds do most new-born babies make?

Which is the most common vowel sound?

4. The earliest sounds made by a new-born babe are monosyllabic cries. During the first few days of life the infant most frequently gives voice to eight distinguishable sounds, which represent about a fifth of the sound elements used by adults. These eight include only five of about a dozen vowel sounds listed in the International Phonetic Alphabet, and three consonants of a possible two dozen. Its most frequent cry by far is æ, like the vowel in the word fat; this sound amounts to 90 per cent of an infant's vowel *utterances**. In one study involving 40 babies under 10 days of age, it was found to be the only vowel used by all the subjects. The other four early vowel sounds are I as in fit, ɛ as in set, ʌ as in up and u as in food. The three consonants are h, l and the glottal stop, a consonant formed by pressure of the breath behind the closed glottis.

5. Vowels are usually classified into three groups: front, middle, and back, corresponding to the parts of the mouth and tongue used in their phonation. The sound I, as in fit, is a front vowel. The sound u, as in food, is a back vowel. An infant's vowel repertoire consists mostly of front vowels. In its consonant equipment the opposite is usually true: two of the three consonants it uses are phonated by the back mouth parts, namely h and the glottal stop.

How does babbling help speech development?

How long does the babbling phase last?

6. As the infant grows older, non-crying sounds begin to dominate the cries. The soft cooings and utterances that delight parents become more frequent. The child achieves increasing control of the mouth parts for vocalizing back vowels and front consonants—the labials, dentals and postdentals. Then begins a long period of meaningless babbling. Babbling has a real function in speech development; it is a practice period for control of the sound elements of language. The baby seems to be trying out new vowel and consonant combinations in a bewildering array. He repeats these sounds over and over again on varying pitches, with varying intensities and cadences. He mouths them, gets the kinesthetic feel of them with lips, tongue and cheeks, and unconsciously and endlessly practices them. Significantly, after a year of this, meaningful words—at first mere approximations of words—begin to appear upon the background of infantile babbling.

7. Meaningful words appear toward the end of the first year or the beginning of the second year of life. At first they constitute a very small proportion of the infant's vocalization, but during the later part of the second year they become prominent. A word usually passes through an interesting transformation. At first it is a crude approximation. In nurseries the world over, the baby lies in a crib and babbles meaningless sounds such as "mamama" or "adadada." Under the *coaching** of parents, these babblings are abbreviated to "mama" and to "daddy." This is the way one child learned the word milk: at first it was "meme," then "mik mik" and finally milk. Pillow is often pronounced "pido." In the case of another child, the more difficult word please evolved from "be" through the series "ble," "pez," "pwez" to please. Sometimes the first words exhibit an onomatopoeic character. Thus a watch is a "tick tick"; a dog a "bow wow"; and a cow a "moo moo."

What vowel-sound differences exist between boys and girls?

8. There are no fundamental group differences in the inherent phonetic equipment of human beings. in the first 10 days of life, boys and girls, white children and Negroes[1] make pretty much the same sounds. But by the time they begin to form word

1. In a more recent text, the term "black children" would have been used.

patterns, some sex differences do appear. For instance, at a year and a half, girls exceed boys in the ability to use consonants at the beginning, in the middle and at the end of a word. The mean number of consonants used by girls in the initial position is 8.7 as against 7.7 for boys. For the medial position, the mean for girls is 7.9 and for boys 6.9. In the final position, girls use 2.9 consonants while boys use 2.4.

How many words will an average child know at the age of 21 months?

9. The average eight-month-old child is unable to use words. At 10 months he probably will have one word; at 12 months, about three words. At a year and a half, his vocabulary may be 20 words. During the next three months it will jump to over 100, and at two years it may contain as many as 250 words.

One fairly obvious explanation is given for the lower performance of working class children. Can you think of any others?

10. We can study the differences in speech development of infants in different home environments. A comparison of the speech of babies of working-class families with those whose fathers are doctors, lawyers, teachers or business owners is shown in the chart on this page. These curves are based on the frequency criterion of speech development. By this criterion the speech development of babies in homes of workers is considerably below that of the professional group. One suggested explanation is that the experience of the worker's child is more manual, while the environment in the professional household is highly verbal.

11. We have found that low-grade *feeble-minded* * children, that is, idiots and imbeciles, in the fourth year of life possess the speech-sound status of year-old infants. When these chilren were examined a year later, they had made no progress whatever. This degree of speech retardation is practically hopeless.

Scientific American, 1949.

Exercises 1

1. *Pre-reading activities*

a) Look at these words :

- baby
- babe
- suckling
- infant
- toddler

Match them with these descriptions:

- ________ is the scientific name for a human being up to two years old.
- ________ is an archaic term of endearment.

- ________ is still at the breast-feeding stage.
- ________ is the most common term.
- ________ is just beginning to learn how to walk.

b) The text states that, at one year old, a baby "coos" and "babbles". Can you think of any circumstances when we say of an adult that she/he is "cooing" or "babbling"?

c) "There was a "bewildering array" of watches in the jeweller's shop window."
Were there many watches?
Would it be easy to choose one?

2. *Comprehension*

Read paragraphs 1 to 3 quickly, noting down answers to the following questions.
a) What role is played by the nursery of the local obstetric hospital?
b) How often do home visits occur?
c) What happens during each visit?
d) Why is it as important to visit the home of a lawyer as that of a factory worker?
e) How does infant speech development in orphanages or in schools for the mentally handicapped compare with home-raised infants?
f) Why are infant speech development studies carried out in schools for the deaf?
Now continue with the rest of the text, answering the questions alougside.

3. *Text content*

Read paragraph 5 of the text and fill in the diagram below to show where vowels and consonants are formed, noting their names and giving examples of them:

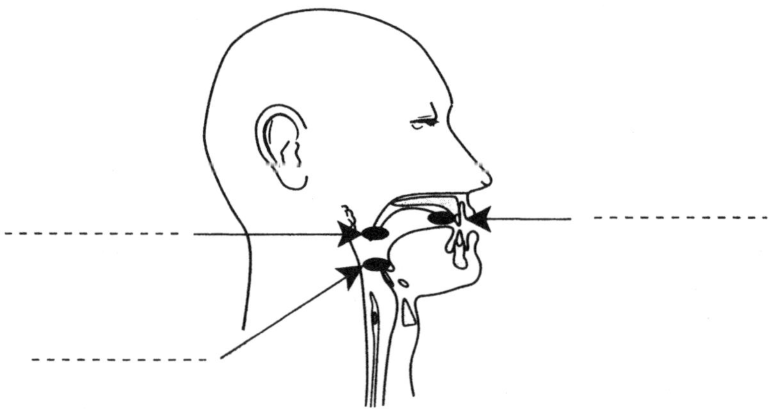

4. *Grammar review*

- **Frequency – indefinite and definite.**

The author makes a number of references to frequency;
Para 4: "the infant most frequently gives voice... "
Para 4: "Its most frequent cry is... "
Para 5: "Vowels are usually classified..."
Para 7: "Sometimes the first words exhibit..."
All these words are of indefinite frequency.

Now look at this excerpt:
Para 2: "it is visited at regular intervals of two weeks or a month..."
This is an example of definite frequency.

You are probably familiar with most of the expressions of definite frequency:

Once an hour/three times per week/every month/yearly, etc.

However, the hierarchy of indefinite frequency is rather more complex:

Always
Nearly always/almost always
Usually/normally/generally
Often/frequently
Sometimes
Occasionally/now and then (informal)
Rarely/seldom
Hardly ever/scarcely ever
Never

We can also use phrases like:
Some days I feel really depressed.
Most weekends we go to the country.
She's visited NewYork *many times.*

- **Exercise**

Rewrite these sentences using expressions of indefinite frequency. (Several answers are possible in certain cases.)

- Every morning he drinks a coffee.
- She visits her sister in Marseille three times a year.
- He sees his parents once every four years.
- Three weeks out of four there is a faculty meeting on Friday.
- They go to the theatre two or three times a year.
- She does not watch television.
- Although she's 97, she's only been in hospital twice in her life.
- Every month she buys the "Scientific American ".

5. *Between the lines*

In the text reference is made to the International Phonemic Alphabet. Here it is:

Letter	Phonemic Transcription
A	ei
B	bi:
C	si:
D	di:
E	i:
F	ef
G	dʒi:
H	eitʃ
I	ai
J	dʒei
K	kei
L	el
M	em
N	en
O	ou
P	pi
Q	kju:
R	a:r (US) a: (UK)
S	es
T	ti:
U	ju:
V	vi:
W	dʌblju
X	eks
Y	wai
Z	zi: (US) zed (UK and Canada)

6. *Discussion*

Read the last paragraph of this text again. Even allowing for the language used (see the remarks in the Commentary on this) the author is extremely pessimistic about the chances of training mentally disabled children to speak.

Has the situation evolved very much since this text was written?

2

Social Attachments in Infancy

S.R. Schaffer and Peggy Emerson, 1964

Until the 1960s Behaviorism reigned supreme. It was based on the principle that behavior patterns are acquired by a conditioning mechanism. Mother-child relationships and tenderness were said to be conditioned only by the act of nutrition, the mother becoming a conditioning stimulus because she is systematically associated with the feeding bottle (as well as the everyday actions which diminish the effects of such unpleasant stimuli as wet nappies, etc.). However, about this period, a series of new concepts were to put these accepted notions of Behaviorism into question.

(Read exercise 1 before reading the text)

1. One reason for the dearth of studies may well lie in the strangle-hold which an almost *universally accepted theory** can sometimes exercise on research. Fortunately, controversy has now been stimulated by two developments: *Harlow's intriguing work** on the infant-mother relationship in the monkey, which casts doubt on the all-important role previously attributed to the infant's feeding experiences in the establishment of affectional bonds (Harlow, 1958, 1961; Harlow and Zimmermann, 1959), and the challenging theory which Bowlby (1958) has advanced to account for the nature and formation of the child's tie to the mother. In his paper Bowlby attacks the *secondary drive theory** of social development, suggesting instead that social tendencies are primary and that a number of *inborn behavior patterns** (such as following, clinging, sucking, smiling and crying) serve to bind the child to the mother from the beginning. To emphasize this change in theoretical orientation he has proposed to drop the term *emotional dependence* and substitute the term *attachment.*

2. Our suggestion is that the core of the attachment function is represented by one of the simplest yet most fundamental elements in social behavior, namely *the tendency of the young to seek the proximity of certain other members of the species.* Approaching attachment in this way, we are dealing with a relatively clear-cut, easily identifiable behavior tendency which may be observed to occur almost universally amongst animals as well as in man. Its biological usefulness in a condition of infantile helplessness is obvious enough to need no further comment. It is likely that we are confronted here with one of the most basic requirements of the young organism to which powerful emotions are linked but to which, in the early stages of development, direct behavioral expression is generally given. Such a fundamental tendency must be isolated, named and studied, and it appears to us that the most economical usage of the term attachment is represented by this tendency.

3. A further advantage of this conception of attachment lies in the linkage which may be made between *proximity seeking* and *proximity avoidance.* Attachments are generally focused on certain specific individuals only, while to others fear responses may be shown. That proximity avoidance (or, as it has been more commonly labeled, fear of strangers or eight-months'-anxiety) is in some way related to proximity seeking has been widely accepted, though, apart from some preliminary suggestions by Benjamin (1959), Freedman (1961) and Spitz (1950) we are still largely ignorant about the details of such interaction.

An operational criterion for attachment

4. Some further examination of the attachment concept is necessary if we are to make suggestions as to how it may most suitably be recognized and assessed. It is well established that, from about the second or third month on, an infant will behave differently with his mother as compared to strangers. He may smile and vocalize at her more readily, he may visually follow her more than he would other people and he is likely to quieten sooner when picked up by her after crying. Perceptual discrimination has thus taken place: the infant is now able to recognize his mother. This is clearly a necessary *precondition* to the formation of an attachment to a specific individual, but the ability to recognize the familiar person cannot, by itself, be regarded as evidence of attachment. Thus, in a study by Schaffer and Callender (Schaffer, 1958; Schaffer and Callender, 1959) of the reactions of infants to hospitalization, evidence of separation protest did not emerge until approximately seven months of age, i.e. long after perceptual discrimination had taken place. The infant who views his mother's absence with equanimity and readily accepts a strange caretaker can hardly be said to have formed an attachment to the former, however readily he may be able to distinguish her from an unfamiliar nurse. To characterize recognition and quicker reactiveness as attachment is thus a highly doubtful supposition. Moreover, all the evidence from studies of smiling (Ahrens, 1954; Spitz and Wolf, 1946) suggests that right up to six to eight months of age the infant is not responding to the adult as another person, i.e. in a characteristic social manner, but is merely reacting to the perception of certain primitive stimulus configurations. That a familiar configuration can elicit a response more speedily and intensely than an unfamiliar one can be readily understood without evoking the concept of attachment.

5. Another precondition appears necessary. If by attachment a particular kind of relationship to a particular kind of object is implied, then one can hardly look for such a relationship until the individual is capable of having the concept of an object. In order to form a permanent bond with another person it is necessary to conceive of this person as an entity apart from the self, with an independent existence in time and space. Attachment involves detachment, and here Piaget's (1953, 1955) demonstration of the stages through which the infant must progress before he can conserve the object becomes highly relevant to the understanding of early social behavior. Up to the third quarter of the first year, Piaget has shown, a state of 'adualism' exists, in which there is no distinction between the self and the environment.

6. As his criterion for object conservation Piaget used the infant's reaction to the departure of an object from the immediate perceptual field. Similarly, we propose to use the separation response of an infant as our operational criterion for the existence of social attachments.

Summary of empirical study

7. The study takes the form of a longitudinal follow-up, in which sixty infants were investigated at four-weekly intervals from the early weeks on up to the end of the first year and again at eighteen months of age. With the use of an attachment scale, based on seven everyday separation situations, the following three main parameters were explored: the age at onset of specific attachments, the intensity of such attachments and the number of objects to whom attachments are formed. A measure of fear of strangers was also included.

8. Results indicate that the age at onset of specific attachments is generally to be found in the third quarter of the first year, but that this is preceded by a phase of indiscriminate attachment behavior; that the intensity of specific attachment increases most in the first month following onset and that thereafter fluctuations occur in individual cases which make long-term prediction difficult; and that multiplicity of objects can be found in some instances at the very beginning of the specific attachment phase, becoming the rule in most of the remaining cases very soon thereafter.

Excerpts from H. R. Schaffer and Peggy E. Emerson, 'The development of social attachments in infancy', *Monographs of the Society for Research in Child Development*, vol. 29, 1964, no. 3.

Exercises 2

1. *Pre-reading activity*

Most people remain emotionally *attached* to their parents long after they are no longer *dependent* on them.
How true is this of domestic animals (*eg* cats) or of other animals?
Is it always true of human beings? Can you think of any exceptions (from your own experience or from any novels or films)?

2. *Vocabulary and comprehension check*

a) Read paragraph 1 only and from their contexts, try to guess at the meaning of the words/expressions below:

- dearth
- to exercise a stranglehold
- to cast doubt
- tie
- to cling
- to suck
- to bind

b) Now answer these questions from paragraph 1

– What has been one of the consequences of the influence of behaviorism?
– How did Harlow's, and later, Bowlby's work stimulate controversy?

3. *Vocabulary and comprehension*

Paragraphs 2 - 9
First link the following words with their meanings:

A. core	1. substitute
B. clear-cut	2. beginning
C. linkage	3. centre
D. caretaker	4. distinct
E. onset	5. connection

A	B	C	D	E

Now choose the best answers to the following:
Para 2: Attachment is represented by a seeking for
a) proximity to others.

b) proximity to the mother.
c) proximity to one's kind.

Para 3: The search for and paradoxical avoidance of proximity is
a) not accepted by Spitz.
b) a commonly-known theory.
c) a preliminary suggestion by Benjamin and Freedman.

Para 4: At three months, a child recognizes its mother
a) but has formed no proven attachment.
b) and has begun to attach itself.
c) and is indifferent to her.

Para 4: In hospital, a 5 or 6 month old child is likely to
a) be indifferent to its nurse.
b) be indifferent to its mother's absence.
c) cry for its mother.

Para 5: At the age of nine months, a child
a) is unable to perceive outside the self.
b) views others as objects.
c) can "detach" itself from its surroundings.

Para 6: How did the authors' experiment and methods compare to those of Piaget?

Para 7: In all, how many parameters were used?

Para 8: At what age does specific attachment increase the most?

4. *Grammar review*

Two-word compound nouns.

These are not as difficult to understand as long compound nouns (dealt with in Appendix One). However, they can pose problems.
A common example of a two-word compound noun is "data collection", meaning, of course, "the collection of data."
Look at the following two-word compound nouns from the text:
Para 4: proximity avoidance
Para 4: separation protest
Para 6: object conservation
Para 6: separation response
Para 7: attachment scale
Para 7: separation situations
Para 8: attachment phase

a) Now translate them. They are not always as easy as "data collection".

b) Now translate the rather badly-worded text below:

"The enormous response phenomenon that followed our recent language appraisal was especially encouraging. However, it is too soon to say whether adequate performance profiles can be established, as the administration procedures were far from satisfactory. Moreover, there was no system of score validation."

5. *Between the lines*

Look at these two sentences:

"It is highly unlikely he will become a racing driver."
"That he will become a racing driver is highly unlikely."

The second is stronger. The contrast between "he" and "becoming a racing driver" is accentuated. Similarly:

"That Mary is intelligent is not in doubt, but does she have the skills to become chairwoman of this committee?"

(Mary's intelligence is admitted, even praised. But doubts remain about her skills in commitee)
Now look at the last sentences of paragraphs 3 and 4 of the text.
Translate them, bearing in mind the "spirit" of this rather complex "That..." construction, how it serves to underline a subtle contrast.

6. *Translate into English*

L'amour est-il un besoin conditionné ?

Si les behavioristes ont eu raison de simplifier la liste des besoins innés en proposant que la plupart des besoins sont au contraire conditionnés, les expériences célèbres de Harry Harlow ont montré que l'attachement pour la mère (l'amour, la tendresse) était chez le petit singe, et donc vraisemblablement chez le bébé, un besoin inné. Sa méthode... le conditionnement !
Les bébés singes sont élevés avec deux mères artificielles différentes, une maman "grillage" et une maman "peluche" recouverte d'un tissu moelleux et chaud. Repartis dans deux groupes, les bébés sont nourris sur l'une ou l'autre mère, grâce à un biberon placé au niveau de la poitrine. Si l'amour était un besoin conditionné par la nourriture, les bébés seraient autant de temps sur la mère artificielle qui les a alimentés, qu'elle soit en fil de fer ou en peluche. Or, il n'en est rien et en situation de test avec la présence des deux mères artificielles (sans biberon), les bébés nourris sur la mère grillage se précipitent dès qu'ils sont rassasiés sur la mère peluche pour passer contre elle autant de temps que les bébés singes nourris par la mère peluche. Le besoin d'un contact doux et chaleureux est inné et c'est sans doute en cela que réside l'attrait de beaucoup d'enfants pour les peluches, le petit nounours de notre enfance...

7. *Activity*

This text, written in 1964, implies that the "nature-nurture" debate is still with us.
In small groups, make notes then prepare mini-presentations on:
What can happen to a child if its natural attachments are deficient? How can the nurturing role of the state be improved? Can we envisage a period in the future when "nurtured" institutional attachments can be made a fruitful as "natural" attachments (to the mother)?

Text A

Discrimination of Depth in Premotor Infants

T.G.R. Bower, 1964

How can we study what a child is able to see when it cannot yet speak? Experience of conditioning techniques with animals has shown how these same techniques may be used with babies.

Before this, motor perception in the child was studied indirectly (i.e. *if it stopped just in front of a hole—a glass pane preventing any accident—it was assumed the baby could perceive depth). The prevailing theory was that depth perception was acquired during the natural development of the motor facilities. Bower shows that perception of depth and shape of objects occurs earlier.*

(Do exercise 1 before reading the text)

1. Nine infants aged 70-85 days at testing were used as subjects. Testing and training took place in an experimental room bare of furniture save that described below. The walls of the room were coarsely *textured** brick. The infants lay in a crib inclined at 45° to the brown wooden table on which it stood. The infants' heads were clasped between two yielding pads, the left hand one of which contained a microswitch whose closing operated an event recorder placed below the table. Immediately in front of the crib was a gap in the table beneath which an experimenter was positioned. When the event recorder closed, the experimenter emerged from below the table and *peek-a-booed** at the infant for 15 sec. and then subsided out of sight once more. Three ft from the infant on the table was placed a white paper cube 12 x 12 x 12 in, which served as *conditioned stimulus**. The experimenter was able to introduce a screen from below in front of the crib for timeouts, changing the stimuli, etc. The cube thus served as a conditioned stimulus, the leftward head turn as an operant response and the peek-a-boo as reinforcement.

2. Initially a discrimination between cube present and cube absent was trained. Then head turning was shaped in half-hour sessions to a criterion of *VR 5** for one experimental hour, with 15-sec. timeouts every minute.

3. *Generalization testing** was conducted in the following way. Four generalization presentations were used. (1) 12 in cube at 3 ft distance. (2) 12 in cube at 9 ft distance. (3) 36 in cube at 3 ft distance. (4) 36 in cube at 9 ft distance. Each was presented for four 30 sec. periods in *counterbalanced order**. Number of responses given to each was tallied.

From *Psychonomic Science*, 1964, 1, 368

1. *Vocabulary*

There are four difficult words in this text:	They mean:
bare	– unadorned
to clasp	– to hold tightly
yielding	– soft (in this case)
timeouts	– rest periods

2. *Comprehension*

Look at this drawing while reading the text and note what is referred to by the letters a, b etc.

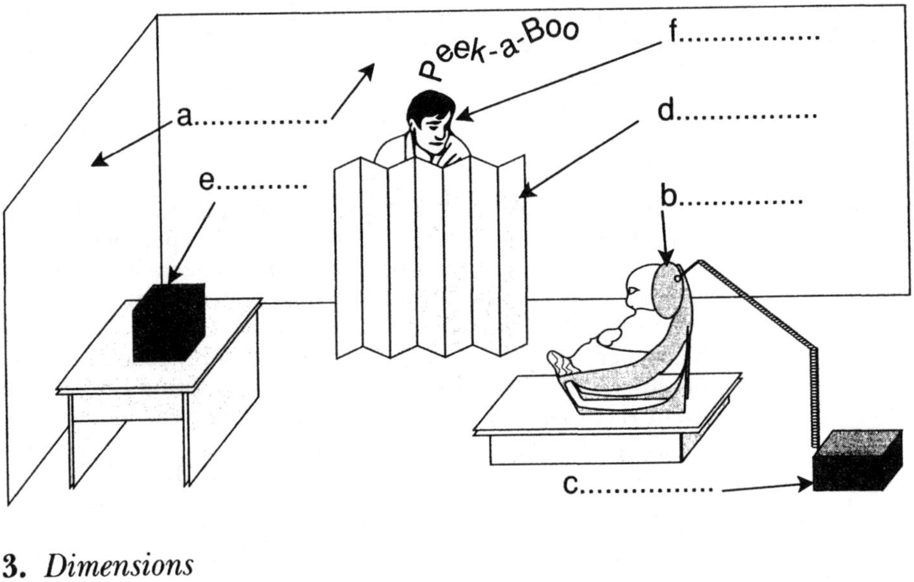

3. *Dimensions*

In the text (paragraph 1) mention is made of the dimensions of a white paper cube (12 x 12 x12). Dimension words in English can cause problems. Look at this sentence:

"The swimming pool is 50 metres long"

This can be rewritten as:

"The swimming pool has a length of 50 metres"

– *Now transform the following sentences in a similar manner:*

a) The road is 10 metres wide.
b) The building is 40 metres high.

c) The lake is 15 metres deep.
d) The wall is 50 cm thick.

– *Look at these equivalences of metric lineal measures:*

1 Inch (in) = 0.0254 m
1 Foot (ft) = 0.3048 m
1 Yard (yd) = 0.9144 m
1 Mile (m) = 1 609.344 m

Text B

The Follow-Up Study of Adult Achievement

Harold Skeels, July 1949

Harold Skeels was both a psychologist and head of a child protection agency in Iowa (equivalent to the DASS in France). He led early research into the effects of early education. His best-known study involved the transfer of a group of disadvantaged children from an orphanage to a specialized institute. Compared to a group of normally developed children who stayed in the orphanage, this experimental group made enormous progress while the group in the orphanage regressed in a few years. But does this early educative influence last in the long term? To find out, twenty years after the experiment, Skeels set out to try to find the now-adult children of the experimental group.

(Do question 1 before reading the text)

1. The purpose of this *follow-up study** was to obtain answers to a few very simple questions: What happened to the two groups of children when they became adults? How were the differences in mental growth in childhood reflected in adult achievement and adjustment? Were the two divergent pathways maintained or did they converge over the years? Were there significant changes indicating improvement or *regression** within and between groups? Was there a relation between adult status and such factors as social history, health history, or environmental experiences?

2. The adult follow-up study began 20 years after the post-experimental follow-up (Skeels & Skodak, 1965). The initial task was to locate and obtain information on every single case in the two groups.

3. Three essential qualities determine the success of locating the subjects of an in-the-field follow-up study: flexibility, ingenuity, and tenacity. The conclusion was reached that ordinary citizens should not try to disappear—they can always be located through patient effort.

4. Some quotations from the investigator's trip reports illustrate the ingenuity and tenacity that were employed in searching for the subjects in this study. Names and places have been changed for obvious reasons.

5. On October 6, I flew from Des Moines to Hawk City, and picked up a rental car to visit several towns to have interviews with adoptive parents and children, and to make inquiry on some cases where we did not have a recent address.

Drove to Sutton, a town of about 1500, to inquire about the Hawkins family. Since they were not listed in Polk's Directory or the telephone directory I surmised that the family no longer lived there.

Stopped at the Post Office and since this was a small rural community, I did not state my mission, but simply said I was with the Public Health Service; that I used to be with the University of Iowa; that I had not been back to Iowa for 14 years; that I was a friend of the Hawkins family and since I was in that part of the country, I was quite anxious to learn where they were. The postmaster thought for a moment and said, "Yes, they moved away from here years ago." I indicated that I had assumed that. He then said, "I think if you will call Hazel Wilford, she can probably tell you their present location."

I telephoned this lady and stated my interest, and she said, "Oh yes, they live at Cambridge, Iowa." She stated that they had moved there many years ago. I then said I believed they had two children, a boy and a girl. "Oh yes," she said, "the boy lives at Holdrege, Minnesota, is married and has two children, and the girl lives in Oklahoma. I don't know the exact address, but she is married and has two children. Oh, wait a minute! My sister says she has three children."

Skeels (HM)
"Adult status of children with contrasting early life experience"
Monographs of the Society for Research in Child Development
1966, *31*, n° 105

1. *Pre-reading activity*

Have you ever tried to locate long-lost acquaintances? What can the problems be?

Look at the clues below and present the problems as you see them, adding any experiences of your own:

- address or job changes
- divorce
- marriage and change of name
- death
- absence of correct information
- rumour
- avoidance

2. *Vocabulary*

Give a definition of:

- pathways
- an in-the-field study
- to surmise

A "location" *means*
❑ a rent
❑ an obligation
❑ a place

3. *Summary*

Summarize this text as follows (maximum 100 words)
- purpose of the study
- qualities necessary to undertake the study
- the chances of success
- how the study was conducted

Text C

The Origins of Fear

Richard Rose and Blaine Ditto, 1983

Fear is often considered as an instinct, but analyses during childhood development have shown that fears are varied and that different fears are felt at different periods. Complicated statistical analyses (not described in this text) can help us make hypotheses about the genetic and environmental factors which determine our fears.

(Do exercises 1 and 2 before reading the text)

How was fear first explained?

1. Developmental studies of common fears have a long research history. Epidemiological, observational, and experimental studies have been conducted to determine the nature, causes, and outcome of childhood and adolescent fears. An early suggestion, recently popularized by sociobiologists, is that our common fears are vestigial expressions of ancestral dangers.

Does G. Stanley Hall agree?

2. Eighty-five years ago, G. Stanley Hall evaluated the self-reported fears of 1,701 students "mostly under 23 years of age." Hall observed that the fears could be grouped into a few categories such as those of animals, water, death, and disease. Noting that a fear of snakes was the most frequently reported fear, he suggested that the relative prevalence of contemporary fears reflects past conditions better than it does current ones. There is, he concluded, "a peculiar *prepotent** quality about some... fears that suggests some... ancient origin" (Hall, 1897, p. 245).

Are Hall's original suppositions probably right?

3. The prepotency that Hall attributed to certain fear stimuli has been studied experimentally by others (Holmes, 1935; Ohman, Erixon, & Lofberg, 1975; Rachman, 1978; Valentine, 1930), and it finds corroboration in results of recent epidemiological surveys (Abe, 1972; Agras, Sylvester, & Oliveau, 1969; Snaith , 1968). Some fears, such as those of snakes and thunderstorms, are far too common to be attributed solely to direct exposure; others, including fears of dentists and electric outlets, are far too rare. A Darwinian hypothesis of biological preparedness (Darwin, 1877) is thus suggested by the data (Marks, 1969; Seligman, 1971). Consistent with that hypothesis is evidence of heritable variation in the intensity of common fears of evolutionary significance (Rose, Miller, Pogue-Geile, & Cardwell, 1981).

What is the difference between adult fears and those of children?

What is the probable role of genetics?

4. Further, the intensity of common fears differs during development: Hall noted that fears of strangers and blood decline with age, while fears of snakes and storms increase. Prevalence data, obtained from a household survey (Agras et al., 1969), provide additional evidence that different fears exhibit different developmental patterns. Some fears, such as those of cemeteries and injections, are common among children and adolescents, but rare in adults. Others, including fears of illness and death, exhibit peak prevalence in later maturity. The factors responsible for such consistent developmental patterns may be quite complex, but it is likely that genetic factors play some role. Evidence that intensities of many common fears vary during development suggests the hypothesis that genetic influences on fearfulness also vary with age. The result: the mixture of environmental and genetic determinants of different dimensions of fear will not be uniform throughout development.

[*Child Development*, 1983, 54, 361-368.

1. *Pre-reading activity*

a) What are you afraid of?

Put the following fears in descending order of importance:

Fire Snakes Heights Insects Death Thunderstorms Dentists
Illness Strangers Cemeteries Flying Skiing Hospitals

and add any private fears you have.
In sub-groups, try to classify them into "private" and "universal" fears.
Do you agree with your partners in the classifications?
Now present the fears of your group (classified) to the rest of your colleagues, giving your reasons.

b) What were you afraid of as a child?

2. *Vocabulary*

What do the following words mean?

- outcome
- vestigial
- household
- peak

Text D

Questions which Clarify

John P. Rickards, 1979

Ernst Rothkopf discovered that adding questions to a text facilitated its comprehension. In the realm of psychopedagogy, where many have searched for the hidden key to scholastic acquisition, this discovery spurred many research projects to explain this phenomenon.

(As the reader can see, this principle has been applied in this book, with comprehension questions placed alongside the texts).

1. By developing an *experimental paradigm* * and some ingenuous experiments within it, Ernst Rothkopf (see, for example, Rothkopf, 1966) created an entire area of educational research, that of adjunct questions.

2. Rothkopf's paradigm consists of interspersing questions in a passage of text contiguous to the material to which they relate. Typically, one or two adjunct questions are inserted either before (prequestions) or after (postquestions) a segment of roughly one or two pages of text, with the total text passage ranging from 1,000 to 5,000 words in length. Questions and text segments appear on separate sheets of paper and the reader is not allowed to turn back to a page once it has been turned, nor allowed to take notes while reading. After reading the entire passage, examination is then made of the amount of questioned (*intentional**) and nonquestioned (*incidental**) passage material retained by the readers. The typical finding in studies of this sort (see Anderson & Biddle, 1975, for a review) is that the prequestion group retains roughly the same amount of material directly questioned as the postquestion group, and that both adjunct question groups retain more of the questioned material than a reading-only control group. This has been called the "direct instructive effect" (Rothkopf, 1966) or more simply the "direct effect" (Anderson & Biddle, 1975). More important, adjunct question studies have generally demonstrated that a postquestion group produces more recall of material not actually questioned than a prequestion group or a reading-only control condition. It is this so-called "mathemagenic" (Rothkopf, 1965) effect or the "indirect effect" (Anderson & Biddle, 1975) which has received the greater degree of empirical attention.

3. The adjunct question paradigm and the associated concept of mathemagenic behavior were born in a climate of *neobehaviorism**, and the early theory and research clearly reflect this heritage. However, in concert with other areas of human learning research, the "*associative model**" (Rothkopf, 1965, p. 194) which served as a basis for the early work with adjunct questions in text has given way to a more cognitive view of learning. This new orientation is demonstrated in the concepts and language Rothkopf (1976) now uses to describe mathemagenic behaviors. Terms such as "selection, mental elaboration and... integrations with previously learned information" (Rothkopf, 1976, p. 116) are all suggestive of this new *cognitive orientation**. Unfortunately, however, further analysis of the concept of "mathemagenic behavior" is not readily achieved due to the amorphous character of the term.

Review of Educational Research
Spring, 1979, Vol. 49, No. 2, Pp. 181-196

1. *Vocabulary*

Give the meanings of these words:

Para 1: ingenuous
Para 2: contiguous
Para 2: segment

Para 3: to achieve
Para 3: amorphous

2. *Comprehension*

(Paragraph 2)

Are the following statements True or False?

a) There was never more than one adjunct question per page of text. (T/F)
b) The readers could not takes notes. (T/F)
c) Comprehension of incidental passages was tested. (T/F)
d) The pre- and post-question groups performed similarly. (T/F)
e) The read-only group performed better. (T/F)
f) The post-question group retained non-essential information better. (T/F)

3. *Activity*

As you can see, adjunct questions have been widely used in this book. Choose a short general text from an English newspaper or magazine and make up your own comprehension questions. They can be:
– True/False questions
– Closed questions (*i.e.* requiring a Yes/No answer)
– Open questions, with Question-words (When, What, etc., requiring a full explanation).
Now, in sub-groups, try out your "exercise" on your colleagues.

Lexique

Associative model : modèle associatif

Le système explicatif des behavioristes était basé sur l'association entre stimulus (et réponses) ce qui aboutit à un modèle associatif de représentations de l'univers mental. L'explication du rôle facilitant des questions est dans le modèle initial (associatif) de connecter des représentations non reliées entre elles.

Coaching : exercer

L'auteur parle de l'apprentissage naturel de l'enfant lorsque les parents dialoguent avec lui.

Cognitive orientation : orientation cognitive

C'est-à-dire un système d'explications en terme de mécanismes cognitifs.

Conditioned stimulus : stimulus conditionné

C'est le cube de 30 cm à 1 mètre (l'étalon) qui est le stimulus conditionné, c'est-à-dire renforcé par le "coucou".

Conterbalanced order : ordre de contrebalancement

Terme de méthodologie qui indique une permutation des événements pour neutraliser des variables parasites (ici l'ordre des cubes qui doit varier pour ne pas être appris).

Experimental paradigm : procédure (on dit aussi paradigme, franglais !) expérimentale.

Feeble-minded : débile, déficient

Quoiqu'employés techniquement, les termes évoquant la déficience deviennent péjoratifs et sont périodiquement renouvelés. Les termes anciens étaient "idiot, imbécile" ; les termes récents sont "déficiency" (déficience) et "disability" (inaptitude).

Follow-up study : étude longitudinale (suivre les mêmes enfants sur une période plus ou moins longue).

Generalization testing : généralisation (au sens du conditionnemnt)

Si la réponse de l'enfant (tourner la tête dans la direction du "coucou" habituel) se généralise, plus le nouveau stimulus (cube) sera semblable au stimulus conditionné (cube de 30 à 1 m) et plus fréquentes seront les réponses de l'enfant (rotation de la tête).

Harlow's intriguing work

C'est le psychologue américain Harlow qui a montré chez les petits singes que la recherche de stimulation douce (amour de la mère) n'était pas conditionnée.

Inborn behavior patterns : comportements innés

Incidental : incident

Il y a apprentissage incident lorsque la consigne invoque un prétexte (corriger des fautes d'orthographe) et que l'on demande après coup le rappel du texte.

Intentional : intentionnel

Il y a apprentissage intentionnel lorsque la consigne dit explicitement d'apprendre.

Neobehaviorism : néobehaviorisme

Élargissement du behaviorisme strict vers les années 50, incluant des variables d'étude (fenêtre entre-ouverte vers les mécanismes mentaux) entre les stimulus et les réponses (ce qui était prohibé dans le behaviorisme strict).

Peek-a-boo : le "coucou" du jeu de cache-cache

L'expérimentateur se cache sous la table et se lève en faisant "coucou". Le coucou est en terme de conditionnement opérant le renforcement positif.

Prepotent : potentiel

Regression : régression

Lorsqu'on étudie un groupe à plusieurs reprises, on ne trouve pas automatiquement les mêmes relations ou écarts entre les membres du groupe (par exemple, le premier et le dernier ne sont pas nécessairement à ces mêmes places) ; on observe en particulier un resserrement des scores autour de la moyenne du groupe, phénomène qu'on appelle la régression à la moyenne.

Secondary drive theory : théorie du besoin secondaire (conditionné)

Textured

Difficilement traduisible en un seul mot ; la texture s'applique au grain et surtout à l'apparence ; on peut traduire par "dont la texture" est en forme de brique. La description de la texture des murs de la pièce est importante car selon une théorie perceptive (Gibson), la texture de l'environnement visuel est l'information de base de la vision.

Universally accepted theory : la théorie behavioriste des besoins conditionnés

Utterances : émissions vocales

VR 5 : Variable Ratio 5

Rapport variable de 5 : programme de conditionnement opérant qui consiste à ne renforcer en moyenne que toutes les 5 bonnes réponses (de façon à éviter l'extinction expérimentale).

Part 5

Social and Occupational Psychology

1

"My Garden's small but the grass is greener"

Leon Festinger, 1962

Psychoanalysis has popularized the concept of conflict, which has given rise to much experimental research into the animal as well as man. Festinger (like Freud earlier) shows how human conflicts are complicated by the intervention of complex cognitive processes. During his research, Festinger discovered that individuals generate different verbal or non-verbal behavior patterns which diminish objective perception of the conflict itself. This, he called "cognitive dissonance", a term which has since become classic.

(Do exercises 1 and 2 before reading the text)

The experiment usually involves buying the rejected toy to pacify the child (True/False)

1. There is an experiment in psychology that you can perform easily in your own home if you have a child three or four years old. Buy two toys that you are fairly sure will be equally attractive to the child. Show them both to him and say: "Here are two nice toys. This one is for you to keep. The other I must give back to the store." You then hand the child the toy that is his to keep and ask: "Which of the two toys do you like better?" Studies have shown that in such a situation most children will tell you they prefer the toy they are to keep.

Why is understanding of post-choice satisfaction important?

2. This response of children seems to conflict with the old saying that the grass is always greener on the other side of the fence. Do adults respond in the same way under similar circumstances or does the adage indeed become true as we grow older? The question is of considerable interest because the adult world is filled with choices and alternative courses of action that are often about equally attractive. When they make a choice of a college or a car or a spouse or a home or a political candidate, do most people remain satisfied with their choice or do they tend to wish they had made a different one? Naturally any choice may turn out to be a bad one on the basis of some objective measurement, but the question is: Does some psychological process come into play immediately after the making of a choice that colors one's attitude, either favorably or unfavorably, towards the decision?

Do adult reactions differ from those of children?

3. To illuminate this question there is another experiment one can do at home, this time using an adult as a subject rather than a child. Buy two presents for your wife, again choosing things you are reasonably sure she will find about *equally attractive**. Find some plausible excuse for having both of them in your possession, show them to your wife and ask her to tell you how attractive each one is to her. After you have obtained a good measurement of attractiveness, tell her that she can have one of them, whichever she chooses. The other you will return to the store. After she has made her choice, ask her once more to evaluate the attractiveness of each of them. If you compare the evaluations of attractiveness before and after the choice, you will probably find that the chosen present has increased in attractiveness and the rejected one decreased.

What is the difference between "cognitive" and "conditioned" dissonance?

4. Such behavior can be explained by a new theory concerning "*cognitive dissonance**." This theory centers around the idea that if a person knows various things that are not psychologically consistent with one another, he will, in a variety of ways, try to make them more consistent. Two items of information that psychologically do not fit together are said to be a dissonant relation to each other. The items of information may be about behavior, feelings, opinions, things in the environment and so on. The word "cognitive" simply emphasizes that the theory deals with relations among items of information.

How can people become more consistent?

5. Such items can of course be changed. A person can change his opinion; he can change his behavior, thereby changing the information he has about it; he can even distort his perception and his information about the world around him. Changes in items of information that produce or restore consistency are referred to as dissonance-reducing changes.

Scientific American, 1962.

Exercises 1

1. *Pre-reading activity*

Look at these two sayings:

"You can't have your penny and the bun."
"You can't have your cake and eat it."

What do they mean?
Give a French equivalent saying.

2. *Vocabulary*

a) What do we buy children on their birthdays?

b) What is the meaning of the first verb in this sentence?
"Concentration camps have coloured post-war man's image of himself and made him more doubtful about his own perfectibility."

c) Which is the "odd man out"?

shop   store   supermarket   hall   stall
department store   bazaar   emporium

Now point out the differences between these words.

3. *Speed-reading*

You have two minutes to scan this text. Search for the key sentence.

4. *Between the lines*

How would you describe the tone of this article?

Light   Discursive   Formal   Friendly
Sexist   Academic   Pompous   Ironic

Choose extracts from the text to illustrate your choices.

5. *Grammar review*

- **Conditions**

There are several ways of stating conditions in English. Here we will study the simplest (the so-called "Open condition", which we will contrast with more complicated forms in Part Eight, Text One).

Look at these two sentences:

"If it rains, she won't play tennis tomorrow."
"We'll go to the cinema if the weather's bad."

Both are fairly banal, not to say uninteresting sentences. Yet they are the most commonly-used forms when we speak of probable or possible events in an everyday context.

Notice now the grammatical breakdown:

Conditional clause	"Reason" clause
If + present tense	Future tense

(the clauses can be reversed without any change in meaning)

Here the sentence is deliberately simple. But it can be made more complicated without changing the meaning of the conditional clause:

"If it rains, she | may not play tennis" (she doesn't like rain)
| might not
| shouldn't   (she has a cold)
| can't   (because of the weather)

We can also, of course, change the "condition" word:
"I'll give you the job on condition that you work hard."
provided
so long as

"In case there's not enough wind for sailing, we'll visit the maritime museum."

a) Fill in the blanks in the sentences below. Be logical as well as grammatically accurate.

– If he ________ (to drink) any more, he ________ (to feel) ill tomorrow.
– I ________ (to give) you the spare key in case you ________ (to get) home after me.
– Provided they ________ (to lose) their way, they ________ (to arrive) at 6 o'clock.
– So long as the taxi ________ (to arrive) on time, we ________ (to be able to) catch the plane.
– ________ you (to put him up) tonight if he ________ (to miss) the last train?

b) Now return to the text. Look at the following sentences:

Para 1: There is an experiment in psychology that you can perform easily in your own home if you have a child of three or four years old.
Para 3: If you compare the evaluation of attractiveness before and after the choice, you will probably find that the chosen present has increased in attractiveness and the rejected one decreased.
Para 4: ... if a person knows various things that are not psychologically consistent with one another, he will, in a variety of ways, try to make them more consistent.

These are more linguistically sophisticated than the grammatical examples, but in each case the sentences deal with reality rather than hypothesis.
Now translate them into French.

6. *Translate into English*

Mécanismes cognitifs du conflit et arguments de vente.
L'homme est souvent dans des situations de conflit, choix entre deux vêtements, entre deux disques, choix entre deux partis pour le mariage, entre deux emplois... L'expérimentation animale montre que ces conflits sont sources d'oscillations, les fameuses hésitations et sources de tensions internes (le comportement explicite est inhibé mais des réponses végétatives apparaissent). Chez l'homme, ces phénomènes existent mais sont compliqués par des mécanismes cognitifs comme l'avaient vu les premiers les psychanalystes avec les mécanismes de défense. Léon Festinger a notamment montré que l'individu cherche à éviter un écart apparent entre ce qu'il fait et ce qu'il dit ou pense allant même jusqu'à justifier des erreurs ou à persévérer dans un comportement erroné. Les arguments de vente utilisent largement ces mécanismes cognitifs des conflits. Dans la plupart des conflits, il y a égalité entre une attirance pour un produit (un vêtement, un magnétoscope) et le motif de rejet "dépenser l'argent" résumé dans le proverbe "on ne peut avoir le beurre et l'argent du beurre". Très souvent ces arguments de vente sont basés

sur le principe de la diminution de l'intensité du motif de rejet (la peur est plus forte que l'attrait) ; les commerciaux ont inventé plusieurs astuces, le crédit qui consiste à fractionner la somme d'argent (et donc à fractionner l'intensité du motif de rejet), le délai de paiement qui consiste à repousser (après les vacances) la date de la première échéance, la technique du prix d'appel ; une fois sur place, il n'y a plus de produit au prix d'appel mais la dissonance cognitive intervient pour justifier le déplacement inutile, on achète un produit un peu plus cher mais au moins on ne s'est pas déplacé pour rien...

7. *Activity*

Situation: The market town of Greenham is situated in the central southern part of Britain. Although it is rather dilapidated, it receives a small number of foreign tourists in the summer months. Up to now, the town has depended on central government funding to attract new industries, with some success. Employees of multinationals have installed themselves in the more prosperous areas of Greenham, though the largely untrained workforce of the town has not benefited much due to its lack of professional qualifications. As very little municipal investment has taken place over the last few years, the council finds itself in the happy position of having £ 10000 to spend on local amenities. The problem is, how to spend the money.

There are three schemes under discussion:

a) A swimming pool. This is supported by those councillors who are worried about unemployment among the younger population. A swimming pool, they say, will help to encourage sporting activities and give the town a much-needed community spirit.

b) An underground car park. Many of the executives of the multinationals have complained about the difficulty of parking their cars in the town centre, especially during market days. The car park is supported by the more business-oriented councillors.

c) A refurbished town hall. The town hall is in a sad state of repair. An Edwardian edifice, it is much loved by the older councillors who see it as an image of the past glories of the town. They say its present state is deplorable.

Here is a map of the town showing the proposed sites of the three schemes:

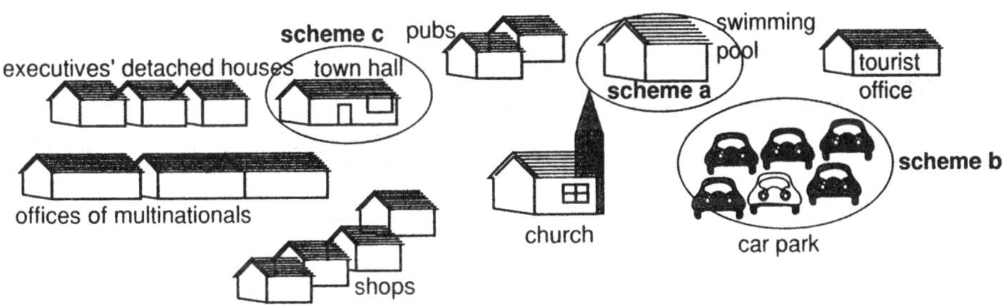

In groups of three (or four, with a chairman/woman) play out the council meeting where the decision has to be taken. Remember, only one scheme may be chosen in its entirety (*i.e.* you are not allowed to swop the site of the swimming pool with the car park, etc.).

After having come to a decision, note down the reasons for that decision.

It is now one year later. As members of the municipal council you have to write a short report describing and justifying your decision (even if you were against it during the meeting). The report must emphasize the advantages and wisdom of the decision.

2

"How to cause discord in three easy lessons"

Muzafer Sherif, 1956

The verification of psychoanalytic notions of conflict has been the source of inspiration of many experiments. Those of social psychologists such as Festinger or Sherif (the author) have ushered in a new field of study—the mechanisms of social behavior. This text gives an idea of the ingeniousness with which Sherif manipulated conditions in order to "make and unmake" groups. It is particularly noticeable that sports competitions, far from being a way a promoting group harmony, are used by Sherif to spread discord.

(Do exercises 1 and 2 before reading the text)

Why were the groups kept apart to begin with?

1. When the two groups in the camp had developed group organization and spirit, we proceeded to the experimental studies of intergroup relations. The groups had had no previous encounters; indeed, in the 1954 camp at Robber's Cave the two groups came in separate buses and were kept apart while each acquired a group feeling.

What was the author's assumption about groups?
How did the author organize his experiments?
What was the result on the group of boys?
Give some examples of how each group reacted towards its rival.
What was this behavior sporadic or did it become generalized?

2. Our working hypothesis was that when two groups have conflicting aims—*i.e.*, when one can achieve its ends only at the expense of the other—their members will become hostile to each other even though the groups are composed of normal well-adjusted individuals. There is a corollary to this assumption which we shall consider later. To produce friction between the groups of boys we arranged a tournament of games: baseball, touch football, a tug-of-war, a treasure hunt and so on. The tournament started in a spirit of good sportsmanship. But as it progressed good feeling soon evaporated. The members of each group began to call their rivals "stinkers," "sneaks" and "cheaters." They refused to have anything more to do with individuals in the opposing group. The boys in the 1949 camp turned against buddies whom they had chosen as "best friends" when they first arrived at the camp. A large proportion of the boys in each group gave negative ratings to all the boys in the other. The rival groups made threatening posters and planned raids, collecting secret hoards of green apples for ammunition.

In the Robber's Cave camp the Eagles, after a defeat in a tournament game, burned a banner left behind by the Rattlers; the next morning the Rattlers seized the Eagles' flag when they arrived on the athletic field. From that time on name-calling, scuffles and raids were the rule of the day.

We are told that group solidarity increased. Was this true for all group members?

How was this solidarity limited?

3. Within each group, of course, solidarity increased. There were changes: one group deposed its leader because he could not "take it" in the contests with the adversary; another group overnight made something of a hero of a big boy who had previously been regarded as a bully. But morale and cooperativeness within the group became stronger. It is noteworthy that this heightening of cooperativeness and generally *democratic behavior** did not carry over to the group's relations with other groups.

How did the author try to produce harmony among the groups?

Was he successful? Give examples.

4. We now turned to the other side of the problem: How can two groups in conflict be brought into harmony? We first undertook to test the theory that pleasant social contacts between members of conflicting groups will reduce friction between them. In the 1954 camp we brought the hostile Rattlers and Eagles together for social events: going to the movies, eating in the same dining room and so on. But far from reducing conflict, these situations only served as opportunities for the rival groups to berate and attack each other. In the dining-hall line they shoved each other aside, and the group that lost the contest for the head of the line shouted "Ladies first!" at the winner. They threw paper, food and vile names at each other at the tables. An Eagle bumped by a Rattler was admonished by his fellow Eagles to brush "the dirt" off his clothes.

What does the author define as "the corollary of our assumption"? How did they decide to continue?

5. We then returned to the corollary of our assumption about the creation of conflict. Just as competition generates friction, working in a common endeavor should promote harmony. It seemed to us, considering group relations in the everyday world, that where harmony between groups is established, the most decisive factor is the existence of "superordinate" goals which have a compelling appeal for both but which neither could achieve without the other. To test this hypothesis experimentally, we created a series of urgent, and natural, situations which challenged our boys.

Describe how "the water problems" was set up.

6. One was a breakdown in the water supply. Water came to our camp in pipes from a tank about a mile away. We arranged to interrupt it and then called the boys together to inform them of the crisis. Both groups promptly volunteered to search the water line for the trouble. They worked together harmoniously, and before the end of the afternoon they had located and corrected the difficulty.

How was "the movie problem" engineered?

7. A similar opportunity offered itself when the boys requested a movie. We told them that the camp could not afford to rent one. The two groups then got together, figured out how much each group would have to contribute, chose the film by a vote and enjoyed the showing together.

And "the truck problem"?

8. One day the two groups went on an outing at a lake some distance away. A large truck was to go to town for food. But

What were the results of these three problems?

Finally, what is a "Robber's Cave" and what are "Eagles" and "Rattlers"?

when everyone was hungry and ready to eat, it developed that the truck would not start (we had taken care of that). The boys got a rope—the same rope they had used in their acrimonious tug-of-war—and all pulled together to start the truck.

9. These joint efforts did not immediately dispel hostility. At first the groups returned to the old bickering and name-calling as soon as the job in hand was finished. But gradually the series of cooperative acts reduced friction and conflict.

Scientific American, 1956

Exercises 2

1. *Pre-reading activity*

There is a saying in English:

"Boys will be boys."

Does this imply
- ❏ hope,
- ❏ resignation, or
- ❏ despair?

What is the equivalent saying in French?
Has the saying any validity?
We could equally say:

"Girls will be girls"

but the popular expression does not exist. Why not, do you think?

2. *Introducing the text – vocabulary*

Although the text is fairly easy to understand "globally", it is likely that a non-native reader will find certain "cultural" difficulties. Try to answer these questions before reading the text.

a) What do you understand by "camp"?
b) *Games.* We know about baseball, but what is: "touch football", "tug-of-war" and "treasure hunt"?
c) *Insults.* If you check the verbs – "to stink, to sneak and to cheat" in a dictionary, you will be able to find approximate equivalents of "stinker, sneaker and cheater."
d) A two-word verb – "to take it". What does this sentence mean: "She was always criticising me. I couldn't take it, so I left her."
e) Now link these verbs to their meanings:

A. to undertake	1. to push aggressively
B. to berate	2. to insult
C. to shove	3. to hit with one's body

D. to bump — 4. to agree to do
E. to dispel — 5. to attenuate

A	B	C	D	E

f) Now put these words into the following sentences:

Buddies Ratings Hoards Scuffles Overnight Bully
Noteworthy Outing Bickering Job-in-hand

- He kept ______ of foodstuffs which he sold on the black market
- It is ______ that none of the delinquents returned to prison
- They went on a short ______ to Versailles
- That couple aren't happy, they're always ______
- My best ______ were my friends in the army
- His performance ______ are high but we doubt his honesty
- When the chief cashier died suddenly, she took on his job ______
- After the match there were ______ among the rival supporters
- Let's do the ______ first and worry about the rest later
- He's a ______, always hitting children smaller than himself

3. *Comprehension*

The "corollary" of the "working hypothesis":
a) Conflicting aims lead to hostility
b) Common endeavour leads to harmony
To test this, the author created "superordinate goals". How does he define these?

4. *Grammar review*

• **The past perfect.**
Look at this chart.

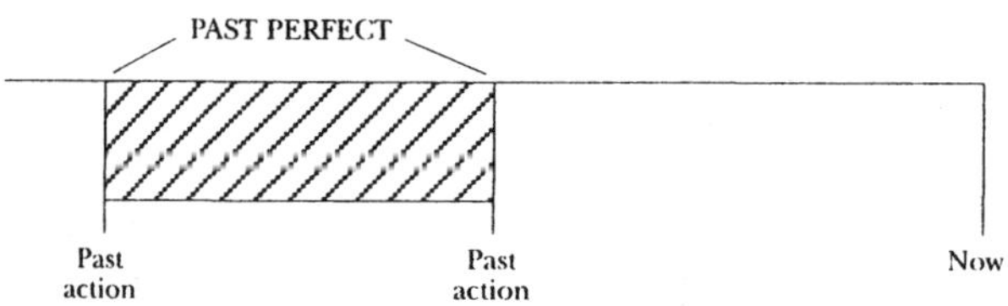

Now read these sentences:

State: The house | was / had been | empty when I bought it

Action: After they | ate / had eaten | dinner they went to the pub

In these cases both pairs of sentences differ very little in meaning. However, it is sometimes important to stress the fact that one past state or action preceded the other.
For example:
– He did not see the sea until he went on holiday to Brighton (perhaps he had seen it at some other period in his life)
– He had not seen the sea until he went on holiday to Brighton (he had never seen the sea in his life before)

a. Add in the most appropriate verb tense (past or past perfect). In some cases both are possible.
Choose the verbs from these in the box:

See	Drive	Know	Suspect	Meet	Work

– "Before he disappeared, ______ you ______ him of stealing funds?"
– She ______ her father after her parents' divorce, then one day he returned.
– He ______ fast all his life without accident until one day he collided with a lorry.
– I ______ never ______ him before, but he kissed me as if we were old friends.
– As the children ______ well during the term, the teachers took them to the cinema.
– He was killed in a motorcycle accident last summer. I him ______ since he was a child.

b) Now read the first five lines of the text:
"When the two groups... previous encounters."
Although they could have been written in the simple past, they would have lost a lot of accuracy.

5. *Between the lines*

Linguistically, this text is interesting in the way that technical terms (*eg* "negative ratings") co-exist with culturally-weighted words (*eg* "buddies", "best friends", etc.)

6. *Discussion*

Perhaps the author's role is questionable. Re-read the second part of paragraph 2 (from "The rival groups..." to "... rule of the day"). We are led to believe that: apples were stolen, banners burned and fights tolerated.
To what degree do you consiser that the author and his associates acted irresponsibly?

7. *Activity*

Now it's your turn to be irresponsible. Think of a group of people you know (family, friends, acquaintances) and work out a situation in which:
– they could be divided into two groups and given conflicting aims (*ie* activities they could perform)
Describe the resultant hostility.
Now give them a common endeavour and describe how this leads to harmony.
Make notes and present your "Experiments in Group Conflict" to your colleagues. (It goes without saying that a sense of humour is vital for this activity).

Text A

Opinions and Social Pressure

Solomon Asch, 1955

Many psychopathological or psychoanalytical problems verified experimentally by American social psychologists have shown that, often, certain behavior patterns were not linked to individual preference but to the influence of social interactions, here termed "suggestibility".

The social interactions cannot be explained simply in terms of linear association (cf the Behaviorists). This is one of the reasons why American social psychology was from its beginning influenced by gestalt theories. Solomon Asch is a representative of this theory and once wrote an article denouncing "the doctrinal tyranny of associationism".

1. That social influences shape every person's practices, judgments and beliefs is a truism to which anyone will readily assent. A child masters his "native" dialect down to the finest nuances; a member of a tribe of cannibals accepts cannibalism as altogether fitting and proper. All the social sciences take their departure from the observation of the profound effects that groups exert on their members. For psychologists, group pressure upon the minds of individuals raises a host of questions they would like to investigate in detail.

Why does the author emphasize the importance of his question?

2. How, and to what extent, do social forces constrain people's opinions and attitudes? This question is especially pertinent in our day. The same epoch that has witnessed the unprecedented technical extension of communication has also brought into existence the deliberate manipulation of opinion and the "engineering of consent." There are many good reasons why, as citizens and as scientists, we should be concerned with studying the ways in which human beings form their opinions and the role that social conditions play.

On what point did Bernheim and Liébeault disagree with Charcot?

How did Bernheim describe hypnosis?

Describe his experiments.

3. Studies of these questions began with the interest in hypnosis aroused by the French physician Jean Martin Charcot (a teacher of Sigmund Freud) toward the end of the 19th century. Charcot believed that only hysterical patients could be fully hypnotized, but this view was soon challenged by two other physicians, Hippolyte Bernheim and A. A. Liébeault, who demonstrated that they could put most people under the hypnotic spell. Bernheim proposed that hypnosis was but an extreme form of a normal psychological process which became known as "suggestibility." It was shown that monotonous reiteration of instructions could induce in normal persons in the waking state

involuntary bodily changes such as swaying or rigidity of the arms, and sensations such as warmth and odor.

How did sociologists use Bernheim's discoveries?

4. It was not long before social thinkers seized upon these discoveries as a basis for explaining numerous social phenomena, from the spread of opinion to the formation of crowds and the following of leaders. The sociologist Gabriel Tarde summed it all up in the aphorism: "Social man is a somnambulist."

The first experiments of social psychologists involved college students. What were the findings of these experiments?

5. When the new discipline of social psychology was born at the beginning of this century, its first experiments were essentially adaptations of the suggestion demonstration. The technique generally followed a simple plan. The subjects, usually college students, were asked to give their opinions or preferences concerning various matters; some time later they were again asked to state their choices, but now they were also informed of the opinions held by authorities or large groups of their peers on the same matters. (Often the alleged consensus was fictitious.) Most of these studies had substantially the same result: confronted with opinions contrary to their own, many subjects apparently shifted their judgments in the direction of the views of the majorities or the experts.

Scientific American, 1955.

1. *Vocabulary*

Read the first paragraph of the text and note down the expressions/verbs meaning:

- many
- to have control of
- a verity
- socially acceptable
- to agree
- completely

NB : "physician" (paragraph 3) in American English is "doctor" in British English.

2. *Discussion*

If college students are susceptible to "suggestibility", can you think of any socio-economic group who would be less so? And why?

Text B

Psychological Mechanisms of Aggression

Albert Bandura, 1979

After decades of Behaviorist hegemony and a few years of cognitivist reaction, psychologists broke out of the mould of "schools" and began to use every theoretical instrument available to explain facts empirically. Thus Bandura developed a theory of social learning, re-using modified concepts of reinforcement and modelling. This theory synthesized conditioning mechanisms (reinforcement, stimulus discrimination...) with cognitive mechanisms (anticipation of reinforcement, denomination...) and extremely complex behavior patterns such as aggression, which cannot be reduced to simple instinct.

Aggression is generally defined as behavior that results in personal injury and physical destruction...

...

Disputes over the labeling of aggressive acts assume special significance in the case of collective behavior involving dissident and institutionally sanctioned aggression. Agencies of government are entrusted with considerable rewarding and coercive power. Either of these sources of power can be misused to produce detrimental social effects. Punitive and coercive means of control may be employed to maintain inequitable systems, to suppress legitimate dissent, and to victimize disadvantaged segments of society. People can similarly be harmed both physically and socially by arbitrary denial or discriminative administration of beneficial resources to which they are entitled.

Just as not all individual acts that produce injury are necessarily aggressive, nor are all institutional practices that cause harm expressions of aggression. Some social practices instituted with well-meaning intent create detrimental consequences that were unforeseen. Others are performed routinely and thoughtlessly through established custom. Judgments of institutional aggression are likely to be made terms of indicants of injurious intent, deliberate negligence, and unwillingness to rectify detrimental conditions.

Dissident aggression is also judged in large part on the basis of factors external to the behavior. Some of these include the perceived legitimacy of the grievances, the appropriateness of coercive tactics, the professed aims and credibility of the challengers, and the ideological allegiances of the judges (Bandura

1973). People vary markedly in their perceptions of aggression for social control and for social change (Blumenthal *et al.* 1972). The more advantaged citizenry tend to view even extreme levels of violence for social control as lawful discharges of duty, whereas disadvantaged members regard such practices as expressions of institutional aggression. Conversely, aggression for social change, and even group protest without injury, is judged as violence by patriots of the system but not by dissidents. Thus, in conflicts of power, one person's violence is another person's benevolence. Whether a particular form of aggression is regarded as adaptive or destructive depends on who bears the consequences. As this brief review suggests, factors influencing the social labeling of different forms of injurious behavior merit more systematic investigation than they have received to date.

A complete theory of aggression must explain how aggressive patterns are developed, what provokes people to behave aggressively, and what sustains such actions after they have been initiated.

In M. von Cranach K. Foppa, W. Lepenies, & D. Ploog (Eds.),
Human ethology: Claims and limits of a new discipline.
Cambridge: Cambridge University Press, 1979.

1. *Vocabulary*

Match these words to their meanings with reference to the context:

A. injury	1. noticeably
B. labeling	2. up till now
C. rewarding	3. schemas
D. segments	4. compensatory
E. denial	5. wounding
F. unforeseen	6. disinclination
G. unwillingness	7. denomination
H. markedly	8. accomplishment
I. discharges	9. refusal
J. bear	10. sections
K. to date	11. unexpected
L. patterns	12. carry

A	B	C	D	E	F	G	H	I	J	K	L

2. *Comprehension*

a) Read each paragraph in turn and choose the sentence which summarizes it best.

Paragraph 1

- ❑ Misuse of government power causes social harm
- ❑ The coercive power of governments is stronger than their power to reward
- ❑ Governments sometimes misuse their powers

Paragraph 2

- ❑ Well-meaning institutional practices sometimes cause harm
- ❑ Detrimental conditions are left unchanged due to institutional aggression
- ❑ Social practices performed routinely lead to aggression

Paragraphs 3 and 4

- ❑ People judge the legitimacy of aggression according to its level of violence
- ❑ People's opinions are self-interested when judging the legitimacy of personal or institutional aggression
- ❑ It is considered unpatriotic to press social change in times of power conflicts

b) In paragraph 3 of the text, which sentence summarizes the author's argument?

3. *Grammar note*

- **Prefixes and suffixes.**

There are a large number of words with pre- and suffixes in the text. As an example, look at this word:

Unforeseen

We can break it down as follows:

UN – not
FORE – "in the future"
SEEN – in this sense "planned"
("Foreseen", of course, means "expected".)

Now go through the text, underlining and analyzing these words.

Text C

"Do you keep your eyes on the road when driving?"

Motoharu Sato and Michiaki Kondo, 1989

Occupational psychology brings together many sectors of activity, as varied as the notion of occupation itself. Its implications reach into more specific zones—ergonomics, organizations and commercial activities. This is the first text corresponding to ergonomy—in other words, the adaptation of man to machines or to his environment. The example chosen is simple enough—driving a car. But as we shall see, the ergonomics are complex.

(Do exercise 1 before reading the text)

Why is eye movement vital when driving?

1. We continually perceive the visual world by *moving eyes**, heads, and bodies. Car drivers receive visual information for driving primarily via eye and head movements, because body movements is restricted within the seat of the vehicle.

In approaching an intersection, a driver's eyes move:
a) left - fix - gaze - fix - right
b) right - gaze - fix - gaze - left
c) left - gaze - fix - right - gaze

When turning right a driver's gaze is more frequently right-oriented.
(True/False)

In general, drivers are less likely to make errors when turning right than left.
(True/False)

2. The results show that there are both similarities and differences in visual search behaviors involved in driving large and small vehicles. Concerning the similarities, there are two typical features. First, in approaching an intersection, a characteristic repeating sequence of eye-head movements is seen: a *saccadic gaze movement** to the right or left, a short period during which eye position is fixed, a saccadic gaze movement into the opposite direction, another *eye fixation**, followed by another saccadic gaze movement, and so on. This repeating pattern of saccadic gaze movements and fixations seems to reflect the visual-search behavior necessary to ensure safety in turning through an intersection. Second, as shown in the interaction of the direction of turning the direction of the gaze movement, the saccadic gaze movement in the same direction as that of the turning vehicle, in turning the curve, is more frequent than that in the opposite direction. This result is consistent with Shinar, *et al.* (1977). They recorded eye movements during curve driving and found that the eye fixated continuously at the road edge. This result seems to reflect the *visual-search** behavior in processing the *anticipatory** visual information for the vehicle control. Moreover, as shown in Table 1, the number of *rightward** gaze movements on the right-turn trials is greater than that of leftward

ones in the left-turn trials. This did not occur in approaching but in turning. This result reflected the difference between the running distances in right- and left-turning.

Perceptual and Motor Skills, 1989, 68, 19-25.

Pre-reading activity

a) Do you drive? Do you consider yourself a safe driver?

b) Where do you look in the following circumstances?
- approaching a roundabout
- approaching an intersection
- backing out of a garage
- leaving a parking space
- as the lights turn from amber to green

In answering these questions, be careful to use the correct prepositions (to – in – out of – into – through – at – across – in front of — behind – sideways).

c) Now make sentences using all these prepositions in the contexts of riding a bicycle, making an omelette or building a garage etc.

Text D

"Is there a hierarchy of needs?"

Mahmoud A. Wahba and Lawrence G. Bridwell, 1976

Maslow's theory was extremely influential in the fields of occupational and organizational psychology. It was only after its first success that many authors began to question its psychological validity. Since that time a number of problems have been raised (described in the first part of this text). The second part of the text is not simple, but gives a good indication of the diversity of vocabulary in this field, caused by the variety of its theoretical influences.

1. Maslow's Need Hierarchy theory (1943, 1954, 1970) presents the student of work *motivation** with an interesting paradox: The theory is widely accepted, but there is little research evidence to support it. Since Maslow first published his theory 30 years ago, it has become one of the most popular theories of motivation in the management and organizational behavior literature. The theory has influenced the writings of many prominent authors in the field of management and organizational behavior. Furthermore, the theory has provided an a priori conceptual framework to explain diverse research findings. Such widespread acceptance of the Need Hierarchy Theory is rather surprising in light of the fact that until the mid-sixties little empirical evidence existed that would support the predictions of the theory especially in the field of industrial and organizational psychology. It has almost become a tradition for writers to point out the discrepancy between the popularity of the theory and the lack of clear and consistent empirical evidence to support it.

2. The most problematic aspect of Maslow's theory, however, is that dealing with the concept of *need** itself. It is not clear what is meant by the concept of need. Does need have a psychological and/or physiological base? Does a need come to existence because of deficiency only or does need always exist even if it is gratified? How can we identify, isolate and measure different needs? There is ample evidence that people seek objects and engage in behavior that are in no way related to the satisfaction of needs. In a discussion of this point Cofer and Apply (1964) concluded that this is probably also true for animals. Vroom (1964) does not use the concept of needs in his discussion of motivation. Lawler (1971) argued that concept of *valence** is related to that of need. e.g., objects acquire valence because of their *instrumentality** for meeting the basic needs of people. Lawler, however, limits the use of the term to certain *stimuli** (or *outcomes**) that can be grouped together because they are sought by people. Even if we accept such a limited view of needs, the remaining question should be, why should needs be structured in a fixed hierarchy? Does this hierarchy vary for different people? What happens to the hierarchy over time? How can we have a fixed hierarchy when behavior is *multidetermined**?

Organizational behavior and human performance 15, 212-240 (1976)

1. *Vocabulary*

Despite the large number of technical expressions used (explained in the Commentary) this text is not difficult to understand.
However, three words may need clarification:

	Meaning
– widespread	– general
– in light of	– "bearing in mind"
to point out	– to underline / to emphasize

2. *Comprehension*

a) Read *paragraph 1* of the text. Are the authors supporters of Maslow's theory?
Summarize their arguments in one or two sentences.

b) Read the *second paragraph* then answer the questions that follow:

What are the authors' criticisms of Maslow's theory of "need"?
In their opinion, can all of people's actions be explained by "need satisfaction"?
Re-word Lawler's concept of "valence" and "instrumentality" into non-technical English.
Do the authors agree with the concept of a hierarchy of needs? If not, why not?

Lexique

Anticipatory : anticipatrice

En fonction des habitudes du conducteur, le regard se fixe par anticipation sur des parties du champ visuel qui seront informatives.

Cognitive dissonance : dissonance cognitive

C'est dans les années 60 que le terme de cognitif fit son apparition.

Bien qu'il n'apparaisse pas ici absolument nécessaire comme qualificatif de "dissonance" il est ajouté par l'auteur pour montrer qu'il s'agit de processus mentaux symboliques qui ne sont pas réductibles à des conditionnements (les conflits ayant été expérimentalement étudiés jusque là surtout en terme de conditionnements).

Democratic behavior : comportement démocratique

Le terme n'a pas le sens politique habituel mais se réfère à des expériences antérieures du psychologue social, Kurt Lewin, qui a étudié la performance de groupes en fonction de la façon dont ils étaient dirigés : une direction démocratique est la prise de décision collective.

Equally attrative : également attirantes (choses)

Il n'y a conflit qu'entre deux choses (ou buts) également attirantes. Dans le cas contraire, l'individu choisit la chose la plus attirante sans conflit.

Eye fixation : fixation oculaire (plutôt que fixation de l'œil)

Après chaque saccade, les deux yeux font une pause, appelée fixation, qui permet l'enregistrement d'une partie de la scène visuelle (quelques degrés d'angle seulement).

Instrumentality : instrumentalité

Terme d'origine behavioriste (conditionnement opérant) désignant la capacité à produire une réponse ou un comportement. C'est un faux ami car il n'y a pas nécessairement l'usage d'un instrument.

Motivation : motivation

Il existe de nombreux concepts pour désigner le domaine des mécanismes qui nous "poussent" à faire certaines choses, besoins, mobiles (drive) mais il y a un relatif accord pour utiliser le concept de "motivation" comme terme générique.

Moving eyes : "en" bougeant les yeux

La vision n'est pas continue mais est le résultat de mouvements coordonnés des deux yeux qui sautent de place en place.

Multidetermined : pluridéterminé

Un intérêt de la théorie de Maslow est qu'une motivation, au sens courant du terme, peut être pluridéterminée c'est-à-dire recouvrir plusieurs besoins, par exemple l'amour peut être lié à une attirance sexuelle, un besoin de sécurité, la recherche d'une considération sociale ou d'une concordance d'objectifs sociaux.

Need : besoin (synonyme conceptuel de motivation)

Rightward : vers la droite

La plus grande fréquence d'anticipations vers la droite peut s'expliquer par une préférence générale due à la dominance de l'hémisphère cérébral gauche (le champ visuel droit est traité par l'hémisphère opposé), soit par des habitudes de conduites (priorité à droite).

Saccadic gaze movement : mouvement saccadique du regard

Les sauts pendant les mouvements s'appellent les "saccades oculaires"

Stimuli (or outcomes) : stimulus (ou issues)

Dans la théorie des besoins conditionnés, un stimulus ou le résultat d'une réponse, conditionnés, peuvent devenir des objets attirants (créant un besoin ou ayant une valence selon les terminologies)

Valence : valence

Terme d'origine gestaltiste qui signifie une capacité à attirer (avec vraisemblablement l'analogie des valences en chimie); la valence est positive ou négative.

Visual-search : recherche visuelle

Les mouvements des yeux ne sont pas désordonnés mais sont régis selon des stratégies de recherche visuelle.

Part 6

Psychopathology and Psychoanalysis

1

Client-centered Psychotherapy

Carl Rogers, 1952

The genius of great men has often had the effect of stifling other initiatives and—like Watson in general psychology—the teachings of Freud were raised into a dogma. However, once the principle was accepted that certain of our mental mechanisms are unconscious, a number of psychologists such as Carl Rogers (the author) tried to "rehabilitate" the role of the conscious.

Objective studies based on the recordings of interviews demonstrate that the patient is not solely a marionnette of his/her unconscious and that it is his "Self" that guides his evolution through psychotherapy.

(Do exercises 1 and 2 before reading the text).

The relationship between the psychotherapist and his client can be easily analyzed. (True/False/Not stated)

1. It was in 1940 that this way of dealing with people in difficulty began to crystallize in the minds of our group, then at Ohio State University. From the outset we sought to bring a rigorous and objective point of view into psychotherapy. We wished to apply to our work the methods of psychology and the *behavioral sciences**. But how were we to do it? The process of psychotherapy is extremely subtle. Few experiences are more disturbingly complex than the relationship between an individual in need of personal help and the *psychotherapist** who is working with him. Can one measure the warm feeling that the therapist has toward his *client* *? Is it possible to weigh the significance of a client's sobbing or of his long silences, or to gauge the meaning of an emotionally laden flow of words? In the nature of things psychotherapy and its results are subjective and seem immeasurable.

In recording the psychotherapy sessions, the author and his colleagues acted unprofessionally. (True/False/Not stated)

2. Moreover, we lacked even the raw material to study. The voluminous literature of psychiatry and psychoanalysis offers little in the way of objective data on the therapeutic process or the development of patients during treatment. Our first step, therefore, was to begin collecting such material in a form that would permit us to analyze it. We decided to make machine recordings of the sessions with clients. We were told that this was unethical, that no therapist could be genuine while being recorded, that what we proposed would ruin therapy. Nevertheless we recorded, at first single interviews, then the whole series of interviews covering a single case. Today we make dozens of recordings every week at the Counseling Center at the University of Chicago, and the practice has become by no means uncommon in psychotherapy.

Classifying the recorded raw material took a long time. (True / False / Not stated)

3. To analyze the recorded material, we began by establishing categories to classify the client's statements or attitudes. We defined and re-defined these categories until we found that various researchers, working independently, could classify the amorphous, often incoherent statements from the interviews with a high degree of consistency. The instrument was then ready for use.

Analysis of the recorded client statements showed a 100 % success rate. (True / False / Not stated)

4. William Snyder conducted one of our first studies and I can still recall the excitement with which we examined his results. Analyzing the several thousand client statements in six recorded cases, he found that an orderly process was evident in this material. Statements labeled as discussion of "problems" declined steadily from the beginning to the end of counseling, while statements of insight rose irregularly, with an upward spurt at the end. Discussion of plans, decisions and goals remained close to zero during the first half of therapy and increased sharply toward the end.

A positive analysis of the interviews tended to show that the client's self-perception was unimportant in the search for a scientific approach. (True / False / Not stated)

5. Such work as Snyder's, though it now seems crude and inadequate, gave the proof we needed that the unstructured material of the interviews could be measured, that the statements both of the client and of the counselor could be *reliably* * categorized and analyzed. We could thus show that psychotherapy, far from being just "talk," had its own discoverable laws. Also, though we were not then clearly aware of it, the need for reliable categories was forcing us to use the "*internal frame of reference,* *" the client's view, as a basis for a scientific approach. We had to stay close to the client's own perception of his experience, because we could not agree among ourselves as to categories when we made inferences from his statements. Thus we embarked on a search for the laws that prevail in the client's private world of perception, and this has proved a fruitful exploration.

Therapy is viewed as a process of liberating denied experience within a therapeutically controlled environment. (True / False / Not stated)

6. As the work progressed, client-centered therapy developed a theory of personality which is based on the image that a person holds of himself. By this "*concept of self* *" we mean the individual's perceptions of his own characteristics and his relations to others, and the values he attaches to these perceptions. This *conscious scheme* * of the self has a regulatory and guiding influence on behavior. Anxiety and *maladjustment* * occur when it is threatened by a dim *awareness* * of experiences contradictory to it. We view therapy, therefore, as the process by which the structure of the self is relaxed in the safety of the relationship with the therapist, and previously *denied experiences* * are perceived and then integrated into an altered self.

Scientific American, 1952.

Exercises 1

1. *Pre-reading activity*

If you had a personal problem of an intimate nature and you needed sympathetic advice, would you prefer to discuss it with :
- a close friend
- your family doctor
- a trained psychotherapist, or
- a total stranger?

Individually, make a list of the advantages and disadvantages of each possible interlocutor, then discuss your choices in sub-groups.

2. *Vocabulary*

What do the following words mean?

– to sob	❑ to laugh ❑ to smile in a sexy manner ❑ to cry
– emotionally-laden	❑ empty of emotion ❑ emotionally-charged ❑ emotionally sad
– insight	❑ shortsightedness ❑ stupidity ❑ perception
– spurt	❑ a sudden escalation ❑ a contained effervescence ❑ an immediate stop
– dim	❑ clear-cut ❑ vague ❑ light

3. *Comprehension*

Read each paragraph of the text, making notes on the important points. Then summarize orally the author's main arguments from your notes without reference to the text.

4. *Grammar review*

- **The past tense.**

Most of this text is written in the past. Two elements are worthy of note:
- how present and past tenses may coexist in a single text
- irregular forms of verbs in the past

a) Read paragraphs 1 and 2 of the text again, underlining the present and past verbs.

Now underline the irregular past tense verbs
What are their infinitives?

b) Read the following sentence from paragraph 2

"We were told that .... ruin the therapy."
Now rewrite this in the present, taking care of the modal verbs.

c) Now put the following sentences into the past:

- We can state our findings clearly
- She will not hesitate before oposition
- The report is to be published
- He must leave the university
- He does not seek the friendship of others

d) "Interrupted" past state or action. Choose the verbs from the box and fill in these sentences appropriately:

(example: "I was drinking a glass of whisky when the doorbell rang")

fall	rang	play	sink	watch	have	live	lower	wait	meet

- He ______ the television when the telephone ______
- She ______ her future husband when she ______ in Metz
- Consumer spending ______ so the government ______ VAT
- The orchestra ______ while the ship ______
- He ______ a heart attack while he ______ for the bus

5. *Translate into English*

Inconscient ou Conscient?
Une grande découverte de Freud a été celle du déplacement de la libido, le besoin sexuel, centre de la théorie de Freud. Mais quant à dire comme Freud et les psychanalystes que les désirs sexuels non satisfaits sont refoulés dans l'inconscient, c'était un fait de société plus qu'un mécanisme psychologique intemporel et universel. Qu'on en juge par l'abondance des téléphones roses, des vidéo et de la littérature érotique. "Emmanuelle" a longtemps été le film totalisant le plus d'entrées (sorti en 1974, il avoisinait les 2 millions de spectateurs en 1977 devant ... "Le dernier tango à Paris"). La frustration (ou l'accroissement de l'excitation) cohabite très bien avec le conscient. La frustration dans nos riches sociétés occidentales concerne certainement, plus que la libido, la source de tous nos plaisirs... l'argent.

6. *Discussion*

Paragraph 2: recordings of clients' statements. It is perhaps surprising that no mention is made of the client's agreement to have the sessions recorded. Do you think that his/her opinion was asked for?

Would you, if a client, be prepared to have your psychotherapy sessions recorded?
Think of the possible advantages and dangers of such a practice.

7. *Activity*

Imagine you are a psychotherapist. Bearing in mind William Snyder's analysis of his cases (paragraph 4 of the text) how would you plan a series of interviews with clients with the following problems?
Pair activity : First note down the questions you would ask, in chronological order then role-play the interviews with your partner, taking turn to play the psychotherapist and the client.

A—is a middled-aged middle class marketing manager and has suddenly lost his job—a job he valued and which gave him a certain status among his peers and neighbours. He has one daughter at university and two sons, both of whom live abroad. His marriage is fairly stable but he hasn't seen much of his wife in recent years because of business obligations (foreign travel, etc). In fact their last holiday together was three years ago. He has little chance of obtaining an equivalent job due to his age. He has always been active (tennis, sailing) and dreads inactivity. He feels rejected and fears the reactions of this entourage.
B—is a young woman in her thirties and lives in Paris. She has had an interesting career up to now (say, in advertising) and at present holds a post of responsibility. She would like to continue this but, being divorced and having to look after her five-year old son is becoming increasingly difficult. Her ex-husband has remarried and lives in Australia. She is not very close to her family, who live in the provinces and almost all her friends are workplace acquaintances. She feels lonely, but to speak of this to any of her colleagues would provoke mutual embarrassment. Her only interest outside work and her son is reading historical novels.

2

Unconscious Mental Functioning

Joseph Weiss, 1990

Following the work of pioneers such as Rogers and the influence of cognitive theories, many clinicians dissociated themselves from psychoanalysis and attempted to re-interpret human activity in the light of cognitive mechanisms and the processing of—conscious rather than unconscious—information. Similarly, psychopathologists began to test their hypotheses experimentally. This was the revenge of the conscious over the unconscious.

(Do exercise 1 before reading the text).

1. How does psychotherapy work? In the past several years my colleagues and I of the Mount Zion Psychotherapy Research Group in San Francisco have found some surprising answers to this question and to an inseparable, and equally profound, question—namely, how does the unconscious mind function?

What have the author's studies shown as regards patients' unconscious thoughts?

How do patients "use" these unconscious thoughts?

2. It is generally assumed that human beings cannot carry out unconsciously the same kinds of intellectual activities they perform consciously, such as *making plans** and *assessing risks**. Yet our studies of patients in psychotherapy indicate that, in fact, people can unconsciously think, anticipate consequences and make and carry out decisions and plans. What is more, patients enlist theses abilities in the service of working to become well—in the service of gaining control over their irrational beliefs, feelings and behaviors.

How have ideas about unconscious mental functioning been developed and what were the disadvantages of this method?

How has the author tried to counterbalance these disadvantages?

3. Most ideas about unconscious mental functioning and the therapeutic process have been developed by psychotherapists on the basis of clinical impressions, recorded as notes or recalled from memory. This approach has been fruitful for producing new ideas, but it cannot assess their relative value. Hence, the Mount Zion Psychotherapy Research Group, which I co-direct with my colleague Harold Sampson, has gone beyond the clinical method, choosing instead to depend on reliable data and to carry out rigorous, quantitative investigations that are planned in advance to test specific hypotheses.

In the context of the author's research, what is the value of the two Freudian hypotheses?

4. Our studies have focused on comparing the merits of two distinct psychoanalytic (Freudian) hypotheses about the nature of unconscious mental functioning. The two hypotheses can be evaluated empirically because they make distinct, testable predictions about how patients will behave during therapy.

What is the function of the "repression barrier"?
How do "buried impulses" disrupt people's lives?

5. Psychoanalytic theory assumes that, beginning in early childhood, powerful "mental contents" (thoughts and feelings) that are not tolerable to the *conscious self** become buried beneath what may be called a *repression barrier**, which consists of forces that prevent repressed material from reaching awareness. Nevertheless, the buried contents—which Sigmund Freud initially thought consisted mainly of sexual and aggressive *impulses** and later concluded also included beliefs, judgments and such emotions as shame and guilt—continue to influence mood and behavior. They thereby contribute to the symptoms that can propel people into therapy, such as inexplicable depression, unfocused anxiety and maladaptive behaviors that seem to be resistant to conscious control.

Why is the "repression barrier" harmful?
How do "word association" techniques help the therapist to help the patient?

6. Because the repression barrier limits people's conscious knowledge of why they act and feel as they do, thus limiting their control over parts of their personality, a major focus of psychoanalytic therapy is to help patients weaken their repressions and confront repressed material. The therapist asks patients to *free-associate**: to put into words any thougths, images, memories and feelings that enter the mind. Such associations provide clues to the patients' unconscious motivations and concerns. The therapist may then interpret the patients' statements, pointing out what appear to be the underlying wishes, fears, beliefs, guilts or the like. Presumably the therapist's interpretations help patients to gain insight into the effects of the unconscious mind on their conscious thoughts, feelings and behaviors.

7. Competing hypotheses about unconscious mental functioning were assessed by testing the predictions they make about how patients will feel and act while becoming spontaneously aware of an unconscious impulse not previously mentioned by the therapist. The "dynamic" hypothesis holds that an intolerable repressed impulse can become conscious spontaneously in two ways. It can overwhelm the repressive forces, in which case the hypothesis predicts that conflict between the impulse and the repressions it arouses will make patients anxious. The impulse may also become disguised and reach consciousness by escaping notice by the repressive forces. Presumably patients will then feel little anxiety (because the impulse does not come into conflict with the repressions) but will also fail to experience the undisguised impulse vividly. The "control" hypothesis holds that an unconscious impulse will become conscious when patients remove repressions after determining by unconscious reasoning that they can safely experience the impulse. Patients are predicted to feel little anxiety and to experience the undisguised impulse vividly. The author's findings support the control hypothesis.

Scientific American, 1990.

Exercises 2

1. *Verbs*

All the following verbs appear in the text. Fill in the appropriate one in the sentences below. As well as putting them into the right tense, be careful to be logical with the sense (some are affirmative, others negative; some active, others passive)

to enlist	to provide	to be aware of
to gain control	to go beyond	to overwhelm
to focus	to fail	to bury
to remove		

– After the elections last year the People's Party _______ of the country
– Yesterday he _______ with full military honours
– She _______ for her children by working in a bar at nights as well as doing her normal job
– He left the appartment last week but he _______ his furniture yet
– She _______ by the number of letters she received after her husband's death.
– The boys _______ the help of a passing adult to get their football out of the tree
– "What I have to say _______ ordinary praise; the man we honour today was an exceptional human being"
– He _______ the danger and fell into the lake
– She didn't work very hard, so _______ the exam
– He tried _______ his attention on his essay, but couldn't concentrate

2. *Speed check*

The author of this text works at the Mount Zion Psychotherapy Research Group. What is his job there? You have thirty seconds to scan the text.

3. *Comprehension and translation*

(Paragraph 7)

The final paragraph of this text is a good deal harder to understand as it is both linguistically and intellectually more dense. Furthermore, it was originally accompanied by drawings. The paragraph describes different ways that an "intolerable repressed impulse can become conscious" and the effect on the patient.

Now translate this paragraph.

4. *Text content*

Write a summary of the text from notes below, using appropriate linking notions as shown:

Introduction
Human beings not "think" unconsciously

contrast

studies demonstrated untrue

addition

humans use unconscious to get well
Ideas about unconscious mental functioning useful

contrast

Relative value difficult to assess
Studies based on two hypotheses

cause

possibility of verification
Buried forces contained by repression barriers

contrast

effect human behavior
Therapists use word association

purpose

help patient cure him/herself

5. *Grammar review*

- **The present perfect.**

The perfect aspect causes endless difficulties for French readers—for two reasons:

- the equivalent does not exist in French, yet
- it is grammatically similar to the "passé composé"

First of all, look at the diagram below:

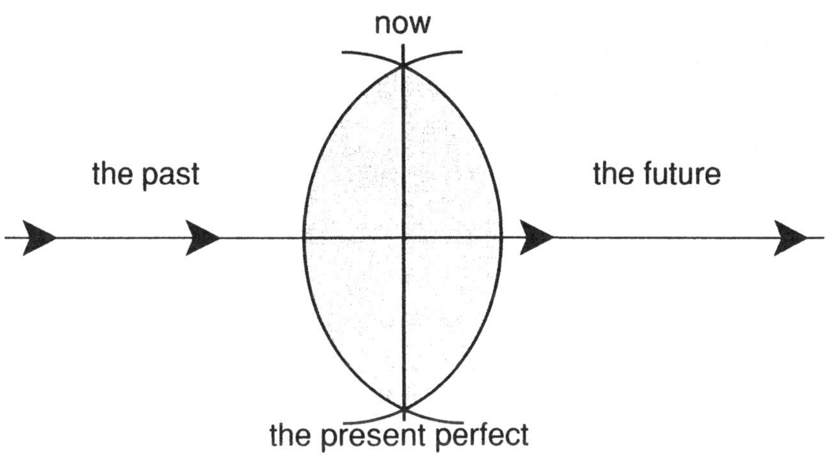

We can see that the present perfect, in some way, links the past with the present. It is used in four main circumstances. Here are some examples:

- He has lived in Paris for five years
- The house has been empty for a long time
- She has visited New York
- The children have just arrived

and here are the precise circumstances:

- PAST "ACTION" CONTINUING NOW (He still lives in Paris)
- PAST "STATE" INTO THE PRESENT (The house is probably still empty)
- PAST EXPERIENCE (We don't know where she is now)
- RECENT PAST ACTION WITH PRESENT CONSEQUENCES (So I'll tell them to wash their hands for dinner)

As you can see, the presents perfect is formed as follows:

- the conjugated auxiliary **have** with the past participle of the verb.

Its three forms are:

AFFIRMATIVE: He has washed the car
NEGATIVE: She has not finished the book yet
INTERROGATIVE: Have they done their homework?

In the PASSIVE of the present perfect:

He has painted the house **becomes** *the house has been painted*

When using the perfect aspect we are more interested in the "fact/action/state" than in the "time-when". In other words, if we need to know more information about when things happened, we must use the past. To illustrate this, read the following dialogue:

A. "I've known the Evans family since they moved here."
B. "Oh, when was that?"
A. "In 1972, I think."
B. "And have they always lived in that big house?"
A. "No, when they first came, they lived in a flat near the station."

However, there are a number of adverbial phrases common to the perfect. They are:

- for (duration)
- since (a fixed time in the past linked to the present)
- so far
- up till now
- lately
- recently
- yet
- already

a. Fill in the appropriate verb form (past or present perfect) in the sentences below, choosing your verbs from the box:

VISIT BE (*two times*) HAVE TAKE OFF CLIMB
PLAN STUDY RISE LEAVE

- She ______ at university but ______ before taking a degree.
- Many people ______ Russia in recent years
- He ______ in hospital for three weeks but he ______ an operation yet
- He ______ Mont Blanc last year, and he ______ already ______ his ascent of the Matterhorn next year
- "Look! The plane ______"
- Last year the company ______ in difficulties, but since then production ______ and now things are better

b. Now read paragraph 3 of the text, underlining the verbs in the perfect. In each case, there is a notion of implied continuity of past facts, states or actions.

6. *Activity*

Non-therapeutic word association. In sub-groups, start with a word, for example:

apple
mother
work
love
table

and, as fast as possible (maximum one minute) note down all the words you associate with the base word you have chosen.
Now, *explain* your associations to your colleagues. Can you trace any "association patterns"? Then pass on to another word.

Text A

Projective Tests

Walter Klopfer and Earl Taulbee, 1976

Projective tests, the most famous of which is the ink-blot test of Rorschach, consisted of having the patient interpret ambiguous visual forms or scenes. These interpretations would then become the source from which the clinician tried to identify the mental mechanisms of the patient. However, as interpretations of these tests were largely based on the subjective analysis of the clinician, they were not universally recognized. Many clinicians preferred objective tests based on a measurable performance or on direct patient interviews. It is undeniable that the Rorschach test had a great influence but it is based on mental projection or visuo-verbal transfer mechanisms which are still far from elucidated.

(Do exercise 1 before reading the text)

Will this be the last time that a chapter on projective tests appears in the *Annual Review of Psychology**? Will the *Rorschach** be a *blot** on the history of clinical psychology? If projective techniques are dead, some people don't seem to have gotten the message. There were more than 500 journal articles pertaining to projective techniques during the current review period (1971 through 1974), not including a number of books that have been published as new volumes or revised editions.

Comparing three national surveys (82, 83, 131) of psychological test utilization reported during the period 1947 to 1971, only minor changes are in evidence for the *top ranking** tests. In terms of the number of respondents mentioning use of a particular test, during the decade between the last two surveys the Rorschach dropped in rank from first to second place, replaced by the *Wechsler Adult Intelligence Scale** (WAIS) in the top spot; the *Thematic Apperception Test** (TAT) moved from fourth place to tie with the *Bender-Gestalt** for third; and the Machover *Draw-a-Person test**(DAP) dropped from second to fifth place. This stability of test preference is very significant in view of the fact that during the period covered by the surveys there was a very high turnover rate in the top 20 tests. In contrast with the clinical use of these tests indicated by the above, a greater decline in research use of the tests is implied by data in the recently published *Seventh Mental Measurements Yearbook* (17). Although the percentage of projective test references of all personality test references has dropped significantly during the past few years, the Rorschach is surpassed only by the *Minnesota Multiphasic Personality Inventory** *(MMPI)* in yearly average references (130 vs 240). The TAT has dropped to seventh place with an annual average of 74. In terms of the cumulative total references, the Rorschach, MMPI, and TAT are in the three top spots, accounting for 4202, 3306, and 1534 references, respectively (17).

It appears from this review and those preceding it that tests of a thematic sort often reveal much more about a person's conscious preoccupations and goals than they do about the unconscious. This is also true of the Sentence Completion Test, once considered a projective test but now widely regarded as a **structured interview**. However, it must be granted that the more common and effective procedures for getting conscious data are probably objective inventories and diagnostic interviews. Behavior probably can be measured best by observing it directly, although it appears that certain Rorschach indices are rather effective in predicting behaviors that as yet have not occurred, such as success from psychotherapy. The most attractive use of projective tests for measuring behavior directly is probably a form of interaction testing or consensus administration of the Rorschach (68) and other projective techniques. This has been used in groups, with couples, with families, and with teams of co-workers. It enables the examiner to get simultaneously intrapsychic information based upon the content and style of the projective responses, and at the same time have a direct view of the interaction between people who have real-life relationships.

Annual Review of Psychology, 1976.

1. *Pre-reading activity*

Vocabulary – The language of trends
Look at his fictitious GRAPH

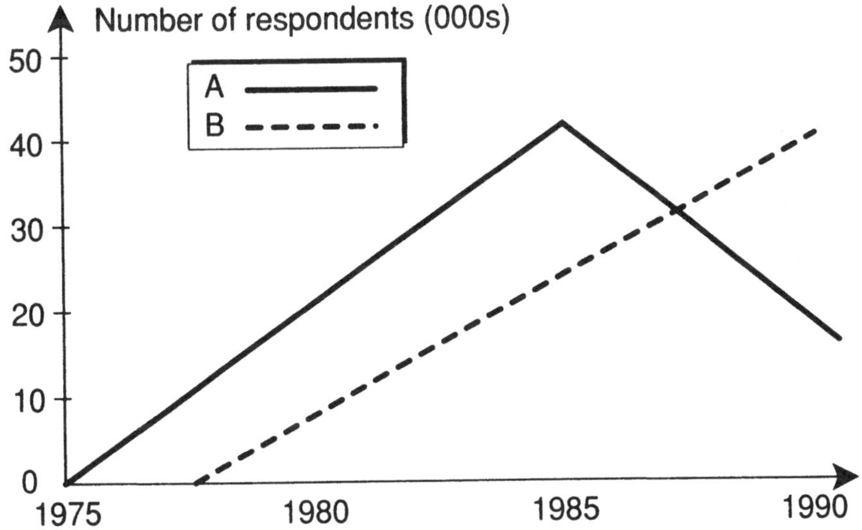

Look at this fictitious graph showing the number of respondents to two tests A and B over a fifteen-year period.

We can say that:

Test A: The number of respondents | went up till 1985, when it
rose
increased
climbed
jumped
* rocketed
* soared

reached a peak of 40 000, then it started | to go down
peaked at
topped
decrease
drop
fall
decline
* plunge
* plummet

Test B: Launched in 1978, this test had a gradual | rise in popularity
climb
increase

until 1988, when both tests tied for a few months. Then test B surpassed test A, which continued its | decrease
fall
decline
etc

NB. those trend words marked with an asterisk (*) are rather more "dramatic" than the others, which are example of common, classic trend language.

Also, note that:

"1971 through 1974" is American usage. In British English we would say "1971 to 1974"

2. *Comprehension*

a) Read *paragraph 1* of the text. Is the tone:

- ❑ Humorous
- ❑ Combative
- ❑ Defensive
- ❑ Academic
- ❑ Resigned

b) Paragraph 2

Fill in this table.

Number of respondents using test
First place:
Second place:

Third place:
Fifth place:
Why was there no fourth place?

c) Paragraph 3:

Are the following statements true or false?

- Thematic tests have limited use in measuring the unconscious (T/F)
- Conscious data cannot be obtained through objective interviews (T/F)
- Rorschach indices can measure future behavior (T/F)
- The Rorschach test can be used with other techniques (T/F)
- These techniques play no role in family therapy (T/F)

Text B

Schizophrenia

Don Jackson, 1962

In this text the author describes the complexities of schizophrenia, its probable biochemical origins, but also its mental, interpersonal and cultural aspects. In the extract he deals with the "aberrations" that result from communication conflicts.

1. Ordinarily a physician treats just one person: his patient. In psychiatry the intimacy of the therapist-patient relation has reinforced tradition. Psychiatrists have been slow to think of the disturbed family that may have produced the disturbed patient. This is not to say that the importance of family relations in the genesis of schizophrenia has gone without recognition. But the early psychoanalytic papers, in accordance with the plot of the Œdipus complex, focused on the patient's relation to his mother and neglected the family system. Many therapists today continue to rely on the "patient's-eye view" of the family and conduct only the most superficial interviews with parents, siblings and, in the case of mature patients, spouses.

2. It was not until the 1950's that therapists began to see the patient's family therapy. At the National Institute of Mental Health, Murray Bowen arranged for families and patients to live together at the hospital; at other institutions the families visit the hospital once or twice a week for sessions of therapy. As might be expected, such experience has encouraged the formulation of new hypotheses. Among these is the "double bind" theory advanced by Gregory Bateson, Jay Haley, John H. Weakland and me, which sees the traumatic situation of the schizophrenic as arising fundamentally from aberration in communication. The "binder," who may be parent or spouse, demands two quite different and mutually contradictory responses from the patient at the same time but on two levels of communication, as by voice and by action. The patient is so dependent on the binder that he is strongly inhibited against acknowledging or pointing out the contradiction; yet he can neither ignore nor fail to respond to this paralyzing injunction. In a model situation, a mother says to her child: "Don't be so obedient!" She thereby places the child in an impossible paradox. If he obeys the injunction, he is disobedient; if he disobeys, he is obedient. In a real situation the contradiction is, of course, covert and arises perhaps from parental hostility that is camouflaged by the external cultural trappings of the parent-child relation.

3. Disorders appear to afflict other members of the family with suspicious frequency just at that time in conjoint family therapy when the patient makes a significant change of the better.

4. These insights from the first tentative steps in family therapy suggest the promise of deeper investigation of the family. There is need especially for longitudinal study of representative families over long periods of time. In cases where schizophrenia develops such study would show not only the character of the family at the time of crisis but also the earlier environment and the patterns of interpersonal relations and personality structure it promoted.

Scientific American, 1962.

1. *Comprehension*

Read the whole text, noting important points. Then answer the following questions:

- What was the psychiatrist's relationship with his/her patient in the past, and how is it changing?
- How do the authors describe the role of the family?
- What is the "double-bind" theory, and how does it function?
- As the patient's state improves during family therapy, what happens to other members of the family?
- What are the author's final recommendations?

2. *Activity*

Discussion. The role of the family.
Is the family dead? (*cf.* David Cooper)
How has the role of the family evolved in the past 40 years, and why?
Have you ever had experience of a "binder"? How did you deal with it?

Text C

Note on some Schizoïd Mechanisms

Melanie Klein, 1946

Melanie Klein (Vienna 1882 — London 1960) was one of the first child psychoanalysts and is still probably the best known. In this text, she summarizes her conception of the first phases of a child's development, centred on schizo-paranoïc then depressive positions. For Klein, problems encountered during the establishment of the second phase of a child's development are the ultimate cause of its later pathology.[1]

I have often expressed my view that *object-relations* * exist from the beginning of life, the first object being the mother's breast which to the child becomes split into a good (gratifying) and bad (frustrating) breast ; this *splitting results in a severance of love and hate* *. I have further suggested that the relation to the first object implies its introjection and projection, and thus from the beginning object-relations are moulded by an interaction between *introjection* * and *projection* *, between internal and external objects and situations. These processes participate in the building up of the *ego* * and *superego* * and prepare the ground for the onset of the *Œdipus complex* * in the second half of the first year.

From the beginning the destructive impulse is turned against the object and is first expressed in *phantasied oral-sadistic attacks* * on the mother's breast, which soon develop into onslaughts on her body by all sadistic means. The *persecutory* * fears arising from the infant's *oral-sadistic impulses* * to rob the mother's body of its good contents, and from the anal-sadistic impulses to put his excrements into her (including the desire to enter her body in order to control her from within) are of great importance for the development of *paranoia* * and *schizophrenia* *.

This early period (first described as the "*persecutory phase* "*) I later termed "*paranoid position* "*, and held that it precedes the *depressive position* *. If persecutory fears are very strong, and for this reason (among others) the infant cannot work through the

1. les textes C, D, E, sur la psychanalyse ont été choisis et introduits par François Sauvagnat.

paranoid-schizoid position *, the working through* of the depressive position is in turn impeded. This failure may lead to a *regressive reinforcing of persecutory fears* * and strengthen the *fixation-points* * for severe psychoses (that is to say, the group of schizophrenias).

While I assumed that the outcome of the depressive position depends on the working through of the preceding phase, I nevertheless attributed to the depressive position a central rôle in the child's early development. For with the introjection of the object as a whole the infant's object-relation alters fundamentally. The synthesis between the loved and hated aspects of the complete object gives rise to feelings of mourning and guilt which imply vital advances in the infants emotional and intellectual life. This is also a crucial juncture for the choice of neurosis or psychosis. To all these conclusions I still adhere.

The Writings of Melanie Klein, Hogarth Press, Hogarth Press, London, vol. III, pp. 2-3.

1. *Translate into English*

Le vocabulaire de la psychanalyse a été essentiellement mis au point, pour la langue anglaise, par Ernest Jones (biographe de S. Freud) et James Strachey (traducteur des œuvres de S. Freud). Pour traduire le vocabulaire technique psychanalytique, ces auteurs ont le plus souvent créé des termes à partir de racines latines ou grecques, donnant à la psychanalyse un aspect très "spécialisé" qu'elle n'avait pas au départ en allemand (on sait que S. Freud a reçu le prix Goethe de littérature pour la pureté de sa langue). La majorité de la littérature en langue anglaise est d'abord produite en Grande-Bretagne des années 1910 à 1935 environ, puis du fait des persécutions liées au nazisme, le centre de gravité se déplace aux Etats-Unis (où coexistent divers courants issus de la "psychologie du moi"), même si les productions européennes (notamment courant kleinien et lacanien) gardent une place de premier plan.

Text D

Object Relation Theory and Transference

Otto F. Kernberg, 1987

Otto F. Kernberg, an American psychoanalyst of Chilean origin, was trained at the Menninger Clinic in Kansas. He was one of the principal promoters of the theory of the "borderline personality organization". This concerns subjects who, while not actually being psychotic, do present personality problems important enough to necessitate special psychotherapeutic structures based on a modification of classical psychoanalysis. In this text he explains the differences between the neurotic organization and the borderline personality organization.

I have considered the ego, superego, and id the underlying structural organization of the classical *psychoneuroses** and neurotic characters and stressed that at this level the vicissitudes of *impulse-defense configurations** are predominantly expressed as conflicts involving the *three psychic agencies** and external reality. The Œdipus complex is the dominant conflictual constellation that reflects the culmination of the development of sexual and aggressive drives in the context of the representational world of early childhood, and is crucially involved in the consolidation of the superego.

Patients with neurotic personality organization present well-integrated superego, ego, and id structures; within the psychoanalytic situation, the *analysis of resistances** brings about the activation, in the *transference**, first, of relatively global characteristics of these structures and later, the *internalized object relations** of which they are composed. The analysis of *drive derivatives** occurs in the context of the analysis of the relation of the patient's infantile self to significant parental objects as projected onto the analyst.

The borderline personality organization, in contrast, shows a predominance of *preœdipal conflicts** and psychic representations of preœdipal conflicts *condensed** with representations of the œdipal phase. Conflicts are not predominantly *repressed** and therefore *unconsciously dynamic**. Rather, they are expressed in *mutually dissociated ego states** reflecting the defense of primitive dissociation or splitting. The activation of primitive object relations that *predate** the consolidation of ego, superego and id is manifest in the *transference** as apparently chaotic *affect states**, wich have to be analyzed in *sequential steps** (Kernberg, 1984). In summary, I wish only to stress that the approach to the interpretation of the primitive transferences of borderline patients suggested in my earlier work may bring about a transformation of *part object relations** into *total object relations**, of primitive tranferences (largely reflecting stages of development that predate object constancy) into the *advanced transferences** of the œdipal phase.

Psychoanalytic Quarterly, LVI, 1987

Text E

The Function of Language in the Transference

Russel Grigg, 1989

Influenced by anglo-saxon analytical philosophy and by the research of Lacan, the Australian psychoanalyst Russel Grigg (Deakin University, Geelong, Australia) discusses the way that theories of language are used by psychoanalysts.

The nature and function of language itself have proved singularly elusive not only to psychoanalysts but also to the specialist disciplines of linguistics, cognitive science, and philosophy. This means that one has to proceed with caution in applying theories of language to the psychoanalytic context; no theory of language can, it seems to me, be applied literally or directly to Freudian *metapsychology**.

In this context in which the *analysand** is invited to say anything and everything, the analyst acts as a guarantee. His presence is the guarantee that this work of speaking to no end into the void actually means something, even well before he is able to know what it means. It is this very special and delicate arrangement that Lacan sees as the foundation of the phenomena that will ultimately produce the transference in analysis.

The structure of the analytic situation places the analyst in the position of being the listener of a discourse he has solicited from the analysand, requiring the analysand to omit nothing, according to the process of *"free association"*,* though in this respect analysis shares the view that here, as elsewhere, things take place according to strict causal laws. There is a determinism implicit in the *analytic experience** which demands, at the start at least, an act of faith on the part of the analysand.

The position of listener, i.e. the analyst's position, is not passive. Although the analysand is the active member, Lacan insisted that the listener's response, his uptake, or his interpretation, decides not just the sense of what is said but, further, the identity of the speaker. Though it is true of all communication that the interlocutor has the power to decide the *sense** of the speaker's words, outside analysis of this power is shared round a bit since we occupy both locutory and interlocutory positions (i.e. jargon that means we talk to one another). But in psychoanalysis the very structure of the relation is asymmetric since one of the subjects delivers the material and the other listens to it. The listener receives, evaluates and sometimes even interprets it. The analyst's position as interpreter gives him the possibility of being what Lacan calls the master of truth for the subject in analysis.

In analysis there is a question of the truth about oneself. The contract to follow the fundamental rule is undertaken in view of a commitment to this position of looking for the truth about oneself and one's *desire**. The analysand does not however seek this truth within himself but within the analyst in his role as *Other**, as the fundamental listener who decides on the meaning of the subject's discourse. This is why silence is so important, since it must leave enough space for truth to unfold within speech.

Analysis, n°1, 1989, Melbourne center for Psychoanalytic Research, P.O. Box 509, Carlton South, Victoria, Australia 3052

Lexique

Advanced transferences : transferts mieux organisés

Affect states : états affectifs

Analysand : l'analysant (c'est-à-dire le patient)

Analysis of resistances : l'analyse des résistances (sous-entendu : du moi)

Analytic experience : l'expérience psychanalytique (la cure psychanalytique)

Annual Review of Psychology

Revue américaine spécialisée dans les revues par thème : en principe, les grands thèmes sont revus tous les 4 ans (comme les jeux olympiques). Comme ces tests n'ont qu'un fondement empirique, beaucoup avaient prédit leur disparition, raison pour laquelle les auteurs commencent leur article en disant que c'est peut-être la dernière revue.

Anxiety-contents : contenus angoissants

Assessing risks : évaluer des risques

Faire des plans et évaluer des risques font partie des stratégies psychosociales de traitement de l'information ; ils sont par nature des mécanismes qui n'ont rien à voir avec l'inconscient. Cependant, les comportements du patient indiquent, comme l'auteur le montrera, que ses actes sont implicitement guidés par des stratégies mais qui demandent à être contrôlées et explicitées...

Awareness : avertissement (au sens de "informé")

Tout au long de ce texte, Rogers, se démarque de la psychanalyse en créant de nouveaux concepts, "self" ou en employant des termes qui évitent l'utilisation des mots ayant une connotation psychanalytique. Il préfère utiliser le terme de "soi" plutôt que "moi" alors que sa thérapie est basée sur le patient donc sur le "moi" du patient ; bien qu'il emploie le terme de "conscient" ("conscious") il évite soigneusement celui d'inconscient qu'on ne rencontre pas dans le texte et qu'il remplace par "dim awareness" ("vague avertissement").

Behavioral sciences : sciences du comportement

Rogers se réfère ici aux aspects positifs du behaviorisme, c'est-à-dire la recherche de la mesure objective.

Bender-Gestalt
Test d'inspiration gestaltiste basé sur des figures visuo-spatiales complexes.

Blot : tache
Jeu de mot au sujet du test des "taches" d'encre de Rorschach.

Client: patient

"Concept of self" : concept de soi (ou soi-même) ou en franglais "self"
On pourrait traduire "self" par le "moi" mais ce concept est trop marqué par la conception de Freud c'est la raison pour laquelle on le traduit plutôt en français par le concept de "soi". Pour Rogers, on le comprend à travers le texte, le conscient domine, ce qui n'est pas le cas du "moi freudien" tiraillé entre le "çà" et le "surmoi".

Condensed : condensés

Conscious scheme : combinaison (au sens d'organisation) consciente
Rogers énonce de nombreuses catégories de mécanismes dont le patient a conscience, ses perceptions, ses relations avec autrui, ses valeurs, dont la combinaison régule le comportement.

Conscious self : moi conscient

Denied experiences : expériences refusées (rejetées)
Là encore Rogers préfère un terme n'ayant pas de connotation plutôt que le terme de "censuré".

Desire : le désir ; **Demand** : la demande.

Draw-a-person test
Le célèbre test du bonhomme est plutôt appliqué aux enfants à qui l'on demande de dessiner un bonhomme (une famille, etc.)

Drives derivatives : rejetons pulsionnels

(The) ego : le moi ; **the superego** : le surmoi. **The id** : le ça.

Free-associate : associer librement
La technique des associations libres, inventées par l'anglais Galton, a été utilisée, chose rare, à la fois par les behavioristes et les psychanalystes (notamment Jung) mais d'une façon opposée. Si les premiers s'intéressent surtout aux réponses fréquentes, les psychanalystes recherchent à l'inverse les associations sortant de l'ordinaire et qui permettent un éclairage de l'inconscient.

Impulses : impulsions ou "pulsions" dans le langage psychanalytique

Impulse-defense configuration : la configuration pulsion-défense contre la pulsion.

“Internal frame of reference” : cadre interne de référence

Les entretiens du patient ne sont pas classés dans des catégories a priori mais en fonction des thèmes abordés par le patient.

Internalized object relations : relations d'objet internalisées

Introjection : introjection ; **projection :** projection

Making plans : faire des plans

Maladjustement : inadaptation

Metapsychology : la métapsychologie (psychologie des processus inconscients)

Minnesota Multiphasic Personnality Inventory

Test objectif de pathologie et de psychiatrie. Il est très élaboré puisque basé sur environ 400 questions à partir de grands traits de la personnalité normale ou pathologique.

Mutually dissociated ego states : états du moi dissociés entre eux

Object-relations : relations objectales : sous-entendu : fantasmatique : pour Melanie Klein, qui s'oppose là à la position freudienne classique, le nouveau-né n'a jamais au départ une position “autistique”.

Œdipus complex : le complexe d'Œdipe ; **œdipal phase :** phase œdipienne

Other : l'Autre (lieu où se dévoilent les significations)

Paranoia : paranoia.

Part object relations : relations d'objet partielles ; **total object relations :** relations d'objet totales

Persecutory : persécutif

Persecutory phase : phase persécutive ; **paranoid position :** position paranoïde (appelée également **parano-schizoïd position :** position schizo-paranoïde) ; **depressive position :** position dépressive.

Phantasied oral-sadistic attacks : attaques fantasmatiques sadiques-orales. **Oral-sadistic impulses :** impulsions sadiques orales.

(To) predate : attaquer

Preœdipal conflicts : conflits préœdipiens

Psychoneuroses : les psychonévroses. **Neurotic characters :** caractères névrotiques.

Psychotherapist : psychothérapeute

Regressive reinforcing of persecutory fears : renforcement régressif des peurs persécutives. **Fixation-points :** points de fixation.

Reliably : fidèlement
C'est-à-dire qui puisse être également classé (énoncé) dans une même catégorie par un autre psychologue.

Repressed : refoulés.

Repression barrier : barrière répressive (censure psychanalytique)

Rorschach : le "Rorschach"
Le plus célèbre des tests projectifs, le plus étudié et le plus ésotérique, est le test des taches d'encre inventé par Rorschach. Étant donné son succès, on dit tout simplement le Rorschach. Ce test est très controversé et si pour certains, il révèle l'inconscient pour d'autres il reste subjectif...

Schizophrenia : schizophrenie.

Sequential steps : selon une progression séquentielle

This splitting results in a severance of love and hate : ce clivage provoque une séparation de l'amour et de la haine. **Split :** clivé ; **splitting :** clivage (sous-entendu d'un objet fantasmatique entre une partie dévalorisée et une partie idéalisée).

Thematic Apperception Test
Test de perception thématique : test projectif représentant des photographies de scènes ambigües.

Therapist : thérapeute

(The three psychic agencies : les trois instances psychiques (moi, ça, surmoi, qui composent la deuxième topique (en anglais : topography) freudienne.

Top ranking : classement des succès (littéralement les "sommets") Familier en français avec les "Top" musicaux.

Transference :transfert (sous-entendu : des conflits inconscients sur le psychanalyste)

Unconsciously dynamic : relevant d'une dynamique inconsciente.

Wechsler Adult Intelligence Scale
Échelle d'Intelligence pour Adultes de Wechsler (WAIS) : le plus célèbre des tests d'intelligence ; la version pour enfant partage le succès avec le Binet-Simon (voir texte 3.1). Bien entendu, c'est un test objectif et non projectif.

To work through : élaborer, perlaborer.

Part 7

Biological Sciences :

Biology, Neurology, Ethology…

1

Neurotransmitters

Julius Axelrod, 1974 (Nobel Prize 1970)

The discovery of molecules that allow communication between neurons has revolutionized our understanding of the mechanisms of the brain and has helped us to understand the pharmacological mechanisms of drugs in the brain. More recently, serious illnesses such as Parkinson's Disease or the degenerative illness of Huntington have been explained in terms of the "chemistry of communication". Similarly, Alzheimer's Disease appears to be linked to the failure of "factories" which manufacture the acetycholine of the brain. Axelrod also demonstrates how the effect of hallucinogenic drugs, once thought to be controlled by demonic powers, may now be more mundanely due to "false keys" in our sensorial mechanisms.

(Do exercise 1 before reading the text)

1. The brain has billions of nerves that talk to one another by means of neurotransmitters. Neurobiologists are just beginning to unravel the complex biochemistry and physiology of chemical transmission in the brain. Many different neurotransmitters function in brain neurons, but because there are more precise methods of measuring *catecholamines** and *drugs** are available that perturb their formation, storage, release and metabolism, we know more about brain catecholamines than about the other neurotransmitters. Fluorescence photomicrography and drugs that selectively destroy catecholamine-containing nerves have made it possible to locate the noradrenaline, dopamine and serotonin cell bodies and trace the pathways of their axons and nerve endings.

2. The *cell bodies** of the dopamine-containing nerves are in the area of the brain stem called the *substantia nigra**, whence the dopaminergic axons course through the *brain stem**, many of them terminating in the *caudate nucleus**. The dopamine-containing tracts in the caudate nucleus play an important role in the integration of movement.

3. The elucidation of the biochemistry and pharmacology of dopamine in the brain has led to the development of a powerful treatment of a crippling disease, *Parkinsonism**. The Swedish pharmacologist Arvid Carlsson noted in 1959 that when reserpine was given to rats, it sharply reduced the dopamine content of the caudate nucleus in the brain and also caused a *Parkinson-like tremor**. The administration of dopa, a dopamine *precursor** that can get from the blood into the brain more easily than dopamine, reversed the tremors. These findings prompted Oleh Hornykiewicz, who was then working at the University of Vienna, to measure the content of dopamine in the brain of patients who had died of Parkinson's disease. He found that there was virtually no dopamine in the caudate nucleus. The finding led directly to a major therapeutic advance by George C. Cotzias of the Brookhaven National Laboratory: when dopa, the dopamine precursor that can cross the *blood-brain barrier**, is administered, it makes up the dopamine deficiency and effectively relieves the symptoms of Parkinson's disease. This is a good example of how basic research can sometimes lead rapidly to a new treatment for a disease.

4. There are two main nerve tracts containing noradrenaline in the brain, the dorsal and ventral pathways. The cell bodies of the noradrenaline-containing tracts are found in the lower part of the brain in the area called the *locus ceruleus**, or "blue place." Noradrenaline-containing nerve tracts are highly branched and reach many parts of the brain. Among the areas they innervate are the *cerebellum** and the *cerebral cortex**, which are concerned with the fine coordination of movement, alertness and emotion. Another part of the brain innervated by noradrenaline neurons is the *hypothalamus**, which controls many visceral functions of the body such as hunger, thirst, temperature regulation, blood pressure, reproduction and behavior. Manipulation of the noradrenaline levels in the brain can change many of the functions of the hypothalamus, particularly the *"pleasure" centers**. Noradrenaline tracts also appear to be involved in *mood elevation** and depression. Recently nerves containing adrenaline have also been observed in the brain stem. The next few years should show whether theses adrenaline-containing tracts also control emotion, mood and behavior.

5. Drugs have been powerful tools for probing the action of neurotransmitters. As our knowledge concerning neurotransmitters has broadened, so has our understanding of the action of drugs on behavior and on the cardiovascular and motor systems; the two trends have interacted nicely. In the early 1950's pharmacologists recognized that the hallucinogenic agent lysergic acid diethylamine (LSD) not only resembles serotonin in chemical structure but also counteracts some of its pharmacologic actions (by occupying *sites** intended for serotonin). Several workers therefore proposed that serotonin must have something to do with insanity. Other hallucinogenic agents such as mescaline and amphetamine, on the other hand, are related in structure to noradrenaline. In the mid 1950's clinical investigators were learning that chemicals such as *chlorpromazine** could mitigate psychotic behavior, and that *monoamine oxidase inhibitors** and imipramine and related drugs could relieve depression. At about the same time it was observed that reserpine, which was proving valuable not only for hypertension but also for schizophrenia, markedly reduced the levels of noradrenaline and serotonin in the brain. The observations combined to suggest that these drugs exerted their actions on the brain by interfering with neurotransmitters.

Scientific American, 1974.

Exercises 1

1. *Vocabulary*

Many of the technical terms in this text are explained in the Lexique. Nevertheless, certain verbs and phrases may cause difficulty:

a) to unravel : to discover, to solve
to course through : to run through (a liquid)
to innervate : to supply with nerves

b) *Para 1*: whence—from where

c) *Para 4*: nicely—here used in the sense of "precisely"

2. *Comprehension*

Now read paragraph 1 of the text and answer these questions:
- How do nerves in the brain communicate?
- Why do we know more about catecholamines than other neurotransmitters?
- How have the pathways of noradrenalines and other cell bodies been traced?
- What are the functions of certain tracts in the caudate nucleus?

3. *Comprehension*

Now read the rest of the text, making notes on what effect the research on neurotransmitters has had on:

- Parkinson's disease
- the co-ordination of movement
- depression
- insanity
- schizophrenia

and present your findings to your colleagues.

4. *Comprehension*

Now read the text, stopping only at the technical phrases relating to the brain and fill in the *diagram* below:

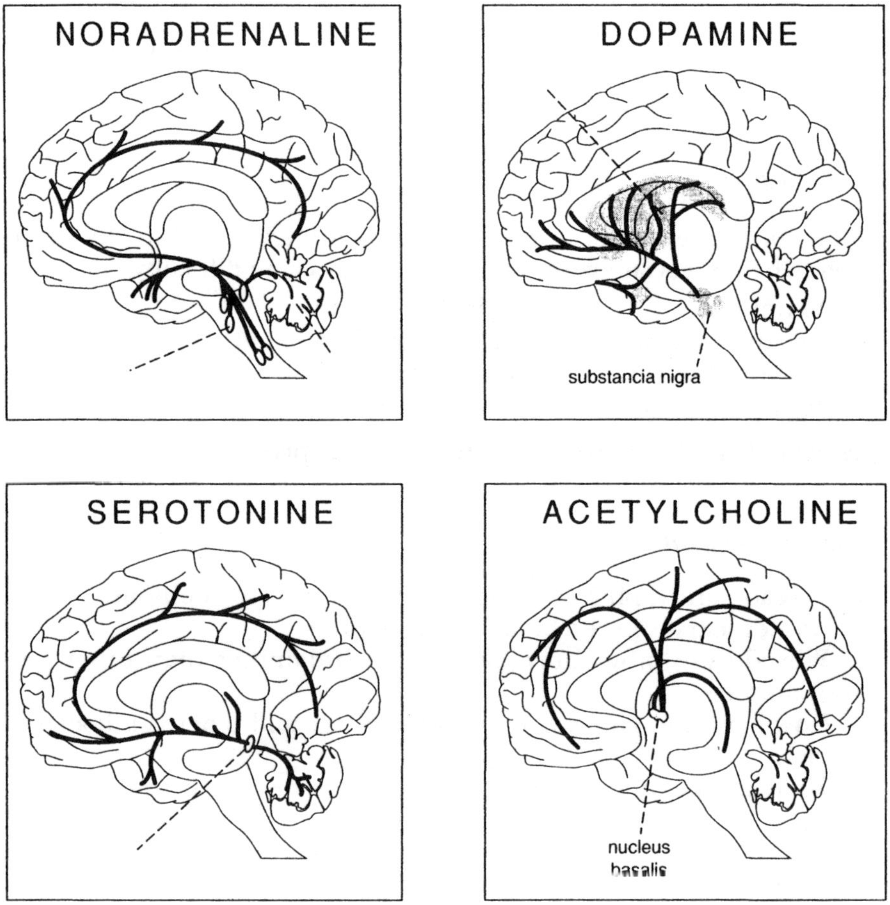

5. *Grammar review*

- **Adverbs of manner.**

The most common way of expressing regular adverbs in English is to add "-ly" to the adjective. For example:

"He is a marvellous football player" becomes
"He plays football marvellously"

As in French, there are, of course the irregulars:

"She is a good driver" becomes
"She drives well"

Other ways of expressing manner are:

"They worked energetically	
"They worked in an energetic way	*to finish the project"*
"The worked with energy	

a) Transform the following sentences as shown.

(*Example*: She made a good speech *becomes* She spoke well)

- He is a slow but careful driver
- They are heavy drinkers
- The committee held a serious debate
- He must do a lot of hard work if he wants to become a doctor
- The new exhibition got an enthusiastic reception
- The band played with more brio than expertise

(Be careful, there are one or two traps here)

b) Now look trough paragraphs 1—4 of the text, underlining the adverbs of manner (there are 8 in all).

6. *Translate into English*

Neurobiologie de l'inhibition

Parallèlement, Freud et Pavlov, l'un à partir des rêves et des lapsus, l'autre à partir des réactions végétatives, faisaient une grande découverte en montrant l'existence d'un mécanisme de blocage des comportements, l'Inhibition. Quelles belles anticipations, grâce à l'observation du rêve, des lapsus humains ou des glandes salivaires. Mais que de chemin parcouru depuis et la neurobiologie montre que les mécanismes biochimiques de l'inhibition sont d'une extraordinaire variété. Par exemple, les neurotransmetteurs appelés catécholamines (noradrenaline, dopamine...) sont inhibés, mangés (ou recaptés), par des enzymes, les Mono-Amine-Oxydases plus connues par leur sigle MAO tandis que pour moduler ces processus (pas assez modulés dans la dépression) existent des Inhibiteurs des MAO, les IMAO. L'identification de ces inhibiteurs a amené une application fondamentale, celle d'antidépresseurs, en psychopharmacologie.

7. *Activity*

Discussion. You have doubtless heard of LSD, mescaline and amphetamine.

Legally available drugs exist, tobacco and alcohol for instance. Why are they legal? And under what conditions could this situation change?

2

Stress and Social Hierarchy

Robert Sapolsky, 1990

Stress appears as one of the fundamental notions of the psychopathology of emotion. Its pathological and psychopathological effects in our daily lives include nausea, diarrhoea and hypertension. Certain social repercussions are essential and some authors have gone so far as to defend the idea of a "golden stress" to explain the professional success of people self-confessedly under stress. Aside from this commercial rather than scientific aspect of psychology, the text describes the different aspects of stress on dominant and subordinate male baboons.

In the next part of his text (not published here) the author describes how rises in the testosterone of the dominant baboons is indirectly triggered off by a high secretion of adrenalin. Thus, dominance is "gold" but not stress...

(Do exercise 1 before reading the text).

1. The year was 1936. Hans Selye, a young physician just starting off in research at Mcgill University in Montreal, had a major problem. He had been injecting rats daily with a chemical extract to determine the extract's effects and had identified consistent changes in the animals: peptic ulcers, atrophy of immune-system tissues and enlargement of the *adrenal glands**. To his surprise, however, the rats in the control group, which had been injected with saline solution alone, showed identical changes.

2. Most scientists would have thrown up their hands at this paradox. Instead Selye focused on what the two groups had in common: the repeated injections. He wondered if the trio of changes he had identified was actually a generalized physiological response to unpleasantness per se.

3. He then tested that idea and found the same three effects regardless of whether rats were made too hot or too cold or were exposed to pathogens, toxins or loud noises. Selye borrowed a term from engineering to describe the body's nonspecific response to an insult. What the rats were undergoing, he decided, was *stress**. Thus, the field of stress physiology was born.

Since Selye's original study, what information have later studies added in the fields of
– hormones
– a person's healh
– people's vulnerability to stress?
What fundamental question is asked at the end of this paragraph?

4. Since 1936 important details have been added to Selye's initial characterization of the stress response, which is now known to involve the secretion of perhaps a dozen hormones and the inhibition of various others. Many studies have also demonstrated that *chronic activation** of the stress response can impair health. Moreover, some people seem to be more vulnerable to stress-related disorders than others. What accounts for the difference in susceptibility? Is it simply that some people are exposed to more stress in their daily lives, or do people actually differ in how their bodies respond to stress?

What is the author's (tentative) answer to this question?

5. I am approaching these questions in an unusual way—by studying stress in *free-ranging baboons**. My ongoing research program has added strong support to a growing body of work suggesting that people's psychological and social characteristics (for example, their emotional makeup, personality and position in society) can profoundly influence their physiological response to stress.

6. When I began studying the olive baboons in 1978, one of my first tasks was to determine whether two baboons exposed to an identical stressor can in fact have different physiological responses. When I considered that a male's rank profoundly influences what he does in a day and how he is treated by others, I began to wonder whether rank might somehow also affect how the males respond to stress. Would the physiological response of dominant and *subordinate** males differ?

7. It turns out that the stress response does differ in the two groups. I have therefore explored the nature of these differences in some detail, along with their possible causes.

Why could "rank" be an important factor in stress among baboons?
Is a baboon's rank fixed throughout its life?
How did the author and his assistant determine the ranks of the baboons?
How were the baboons grouped?

8. Every year I spend three months in Kenya, where I study the baboons according to a standard routine, usually with the help of a Kenyan assistant, Richard Kones. We begin by determining the male's social rank that season, which essentially involves evaluating how often the animals get what they want. For instance, we rate the animals according to whether they win most of their fights, are more often the harasser rather than the harassed, and are able to supplant another male (who might be, say, resting in a desirable spot, feeding or being groomed). I consider males in the top half of the hierarchy to be dominant and those in the bottom half, subordinate.

Why is an anesthetic doubly useful in the author's work?

9. Once the male's social positions are known, I assess their baseline hormone levels and measure their metabolic responses to a physical stressor: anesthesia. I anesthetize the animals by "*darting*"* them with a syringe shot from a blowgun. Before the animals lose consciousness, they become momentarily disoriented, which seems to trigger the stress response. The anesthesia not only stresses the animals, it also makes it possible to obtain repeated blood samples over the course of the day and thus to track changes in the animal's hormone levels.

Are the workings of every physiological system the same for all baboons?
Are dominant baboons

10. With this approach I have found that when the dominance hierarchy is stable (as it usually is), the workings of nearly every physiological system I have examined differ between the dominant and subordinate males. It also turns out that the

likely to suffer more stress than subordinate ones? And in what way is this important for humans? Why is the secretion of testoterone important?

physiological profile of the subordinate animals is closer to the type that is thought to predispose humans to stress-related disease.

11. The hormonal system that controls the secretion of testosterone (the principal reproductive hormone in males) offers a good example of how the stress response differs between dominant and subordinate olive baboons. Although the average resting levels of testosterone are essentially the same in both groups, the levels diverge markedly when the animals are stressed.

12. Testosterone is normally released as the final step in a cascade of hormone secretion that begins at the brain. There, the *hypothalamus** releases a substance known as *luteinizing* hormone-releasing hormone**, which stimulates the *pituitary gland** to release luteinizing hormone. This hormone, in turn, *triggers** the testicular release of testosterone.

What are the differences in reaction after "darting" between the dominant and subordinate males?

13. In both dominant and subordinate baboons, as in human beings and rats, testosterone levels *plummet** in response to stress. Yet the similarity between dominant and subordinate males ends there. After the baboons are darted, the testosterone levels of subordinate males decline promptly, whereas those of dominant males actually rise and remain elevated for perhaps an hour before declining.

How could this difference in reaction help the dominant males? And how could it be harmful to the subordinate ones?

14. Theoretically, the rise in testosterone could give dominant males a survival and social advantage, because the hormone increases the rate at which glucose reaches the muscles. Such changes would be expected to help dominant baboons withstand a physical challenge.

Scientific American, 1990.

Exercises 2

1. *Pre-reading activity*

Stress. What does the word mean to you?
Give some possible examples of stressful situations
- in a city
- in the country

What situations do you personally find stressful?
How does this stress manifest itself physiologically?

2. *Comprehension*

Expressions: *paragraphs 1—3*
a) "He couldn't find a solution so he threw up his hands."
What does this mean?
We can also say: "He threw in the towel" (an expression from boxing)

b) per se. A Latin expression, meaning "in itself"

c) "an insult". In the text this means a "physical intrusion" (eg an injection) and not verbal abuse.

Now read *paragraphs 1—3* of the text, noting the main points. Then make an mini-presentation entitled:

"The birth of stress psychology"

3. *Vocabulary*

Now look back over the text and, from their contexts, try to guess at the meaning of:

Para 4: to impair
Para 5: makeup
Para 7: It turns out that...
Para 8: harasser/harassed
Para 8: to be groomed
Para 9: to track
Para 14: to withstand

4. *Grammar review*

• **Quantifiers.**

As the term suggests, quantifiers deal with quantity. And quantity can be countable or uncountable—therein lies the difficulty.
We say, for example:

a) "Are there many bottles of milk?"—we can count "bottles"

b) "Is there much milk?"—we cannot count "milk"

Let's now look at the scale of quantity.

Study this table:

countable	100 %	**uncountable**
EVERY bottle/ALL the bottles		ALL the milk
MOST OF		MOST OF
MANY (OF)		MUCH (OF)
A LOT OF		A LOT OF (THE)
SOME (OF)		SOME (OF)
A FEW (OF) (the)		A LITTLE (OF) (the)
A SMALL NUMBER OF (the)		A SMALL AMOUNT OF
NOT MANY (OF) (the)		NOT MUCH (OF) (the)
FEW (OF) (the)		LITTLE (OF) (the)
NONE OF the		NONE OF the
NO	0 %	NO

a) Now fill in the appropriate quantifiers in the following interview with a hospital nurse. (Sometimes more than one answer is possible)

A. How long have you worked in this hospital?
B. ______ my working life. I started when I was 18 and now I'm 46.
A. So, thirty years.
B. That's it.
A. And how ______ patients are in your charge?
B. Ten usually. But sometimes there are ______ more. In the winter months.
A. Why is that?
B. Well, ______ the patients are fairly old, as you can see. And ______ of them suffer from cold or malnutrition.
A. But don't the Social Services help?
B. They try, but there's very ______ they can do. Old people are very proud, you see. ______ of them like asking for help.
A. How ______ hours a week do you work?
B. Forty, theoretically. But we have to do ______ overtime to look after the patients properly.
A. And how ______ are you paid?
B. Not ______ . But it's enough to live on.

b. Look at the text. There are a number of quantifiers (see paragraphs 2 and 4). Underline them.

Note also how the quantifier "some" is used in *paragraph 7*. In this case "in some detail" is an understated way of implying "in a lot of detail"

5. *Between the lines*

What do you notice about the difference in style between *paragraphs 1—3* and the rest of the text? Why do you think this is?

6. *Translate into English*

Une échelle de Richter des chocs émotifs 1

Les situations stressantes provoquent une réponse de l'organisme qu'on appelle le syndrome d'adaptation généralisé (SAG, Selye) ou syndrome de "la lutte ou la fuite" si l'on se rapproche des observations éthologistes. La finalité de ces réponses est bénéfique sur le plan phylogénétique, par exemple chez l'animal qui peut fuire ou combattre un agresseur ; mais elle n'est pas toujours bénéfique chez l'homme par suite des contraintes sociales. L'homme socialisé ne peut pas se battre ou fuir si ce n'est symboliquement : l'étudiant ne peut pas se soustraire aux examens, l'employé ne peut agresser son patron. Les recherches ont abouti à une estimation des événements stressants sous forme d'une échelle, en fonction de la gravité décroissante de l'événement, une sorte d'"échelle de Richter" pour les séismes de l'organisme, par exemple :

1. Stress.

décès d'un conjoint
divorce
maladie grave
dispute
changement de responsabilité
déménagement
vacances...

Un événement en haut de l'échelle est très stressant et peut conduire à des maladies mortelles par suite de la chute brutale des barrières immunitaires ou de troubles cardiaques, etc. Mais, et c'est l'importance de la notion de stress, une répétition ou une accumulation de petits événements stressants aboutit au même effet.

7. *Activity*

Portraits of stress

We will consider five people from different backgrounds. A certain amount of information is given to you. In sub-groups, use your imagination to work out how these people could suffer from stress (the situations they find stressful) and what the result of this could be on themselves and their entourages.
If they asked you for advice, what would you say?

A. He is 32, a computer salesman. Happily married with two children. Has a house in the Paris suburbs. Travels a lot. Dynamic, ambitious, ruthless. Has lost touch with his parents. Many friends, mostly from his schooldays, no hobbies.

B. She is 39 and comes from Aix. A family doctor in a poor suburb of Lyon. Married, not very happily, to a financier. Three children. Large pleasant house in a select area of Lyon. Many acquaintances, few close friends. Devoted to her work. Likes sailing.

C. He is 22, a student. Born in Paris, studying in Rennes. Lives with girl-friend, no children. An unhappy, rather strict upbringing in a select arrondissement of Paris. Not fixed on a career, would like to be an actor. Girl-friend (slightly older) an architect. Has ambitious parents and four "successful" brothers and sisters. No hobbies (apart from amateur acting).

D. She is 43, an executive with a multinational company. Was raised in Bordeaux and lives in Paris. Divorced, two children. Has a longstanding relationship with a married man. Is extremely ambitious (often abroad on business trips etc.) Many acquaintances, few friends. Plays tennis in the summer months.

E. He is 64, a farmer. Unmarried, he lives alone in the family farmhouse. Has two nephews who view the farm enviously (but neither is a farmer) Although physically fit, his eyesight is failing. No neighbours, no friends, no hobbies.

Text A

The Bioelectric Signal of the Neuron

Charles F. Stevens, 1979

*Taking electricity as a model, it was once thought that the nerve influx moved along its axon like an electric current to the end of the nerve cell, or neuron. Recent biological and physiological techniques (electronic microscopy, micro-electric physiology and biochemistry) have all demonstrated that this is false. In fact, there is an exchange of ions across certain "gates" of the cell membrane. For students not very familiar with chemical language—an ion is an ionised molecule: in other words, one having one or several electrons too many. A simple example is ordinary salt Na Cl which, dissolved in water gives two ions * Na^+ (the same ion sodium as in the text) and * Cl^- (ion chloride). Other ions, notably potassium play a part in these ionic exchanges which are at the origin of nerve messages.*

(The + signifies a positive electric charge and the – a negative one).*

What is the role of the axon membrane? How is the ionic disequilibrium maintained in the resting state? What happens when the voltage level across the membrane goes down?

1. Axon membrane separates fluids that differ greatly in their content (a disequilibrium). Sodium ions are high outside and potassium ions are high inside. The membrane is penetrated by proteins that act as selective *ionic channels**. In the *resting state**, when no nerve impulse is transmitted, the sodium and potassium channels are closed and an *ion pump** maintains the ionic disequilibrium. If voltage across the membrane is reduced, the sodium channels open and sodium ions enter the axon. An instant later the sodium channels close and the potassium channels open and potassium ions exit the axon. This sequence of events generates the *nerve impulse**.

What does the author mean by "Channels are selectively permeable"? Describe two types of channels.

2. This brief description of the nerve impulse illustrates the importance of channels for the electrical activity of neurons and underscores two fundamental properties of channels: selectivity and gating. I shall discuss these two properties in turn. Channels are selectively permeable and selectivities vary widely. For example, one type of channel lets sodium ions pass through and largely excludes potassium ions, whereas another type of channel does the reverse. The selectivity, however, is seldom absolute. One type of channel that is fairly nonselective allows the passage of about 85 sodium ions for every 100 potassium ions; another more selective type passes only about seven sodium ions for every 100 potassium ions. The first type, known as the *acetylcholine**-activated channel, has a *pore** about .8 nanometer in diameter that is filled with water. The second type, known as the potassium channel, has a much smaller opening and contains less water.

The smaller the ion, the easier it passes through the membrane. (true/false)

3. The sodium ion is about 30 percent smaller than the potassium ion. The exact molecular structure that enables the larger ion to pass through the cell membrane more readily than the smaller one is not known. The general principles that underlie the discrimination, however, are understood. They involve interactions between ions and parts of the channel structure in conjunction with a particular ordering of water molecules within the pore.

Describe the two types of gating mechanism.
A chemically-gated channel responds to voltage changes (true/false)
What is the role of chemically-gated channels?
How are chemically-gated and voltage-gated channels named?

4. The *gating mechanism** that regulates the opening and closing of membrane channels takes two main forms. One type of channel, mentioned above in the description of the nerve impulse, opens and closes in response to voltage differences across the cell membrane; it is therefore said to be *voltage-gated**. A second type of channel is *chemically gated**. Such channels respond only slightly if at all to voltage changes but open when a particular molecule—a transmitter—*binds** to a receptor region on the channel protein. Chemically gated channels are found in the receptive membranes of *synapses** and are responsible for translating the chemical signals produced by *axon terminals** into ion permeability changes during synaptic transmission. It is customary to name chemically gated channels according to their normal transmitter. Hence one speaks of acetylcholine-activated channels or gaba-activated channel (gaba is a gamma-aminobutyric acid.) Voltage-gated channels are generally named for the ion that passes through the channel most readily.

Scientific American, 1979.

Text B

Pleasure Centers

James Olds, 1956

During the 1950s exceptional discoveries about the brain were made by using a new technique – the implantation of micro-electrodes. This made it possible to stimulate specific zones of the brain in order to locate its different behavior centres. Delgado discovered "punishment" centres while Olds (the author) discovered "pleasure" centres.

We now started to localize and quantify the *rewarding effect** in the brain by planting electrodes in all parts of the brain in large numbers of rats. Each rat had a pair of electrodes consisting of insulated silver wires a hundredth of an inch in diameter. The two stimulating tips were only about one 500th of an inch apart. During a test the animal was placed in a Skinner box designed to produce a change response rate of about 10 to 25 *bar-presses per hour**. Each animal was given about six hours of testing with the electric current turned on and one hour with the current off. All responses were *recorded automatically**, and the animal was given a score on the basis of the amount of time it spent stimulating its brain.

When electrodes were implanted in the classical sensory and motor systems, response rates stayed at the chance level of 10 to 25 an hour. In most parts of the *mid-line system**, the response rates rose to levels of from 200 to 5,000 an hour, definitely indicative of a rewarding effect of the electric stimulus. But in some of the lower parts of the mid-line system there was an opposite effect: the animal would press the lever once and never go back. This indicated a *punishing effect** in those areas. They appeared to be the same areas where Delgado, Roberts and Miller at Yale also had discovered the *avoidance effect**—and where Hess and others had found responses of rage and escape.

The animals seemed to experience the strongest reward, or pleasure, from stimulation of areas of the hypothalamus and certain mid-brain nuclei-regions which Hess and others had found to be centers for control of digestive, sexual, excretory and similar processes. Animals with electrodes in these areas would stimulate themselves from 500 to 5,000 times per hour. In the *rhinencephalon** the effects were milder, producing self—stimulation at rates around 200 times per hour.

Electric stimulation in some of these regions actually appeared to be far more rewarding to the animals than an ordinary satisfier such as food. For example, hungry rats ran faster to reach an electric stimulator than they did to reach food. Indeed, a hungry animal often ignored available food in favor of the pleasure of stimulating itself electrically. Some rats with electrodes in these places stimulated their brains more than 2,000 times per hour for 24 consecutive hours!

Why is the electric stimulation so rewarding? We are currently exploring this question, working on the hypothesis that brain stimulation in these regions must excite some of the nerve cells that would be excited by satisfaction of the basic drives—hunger, sex, thirst and so forth. We have looked to see whether some parts of the "reward system" of the brain are specialized; that is, there may be one part for the hunger drive, another for the sex drive, etc.

In experiments on hunger, we have found that an animal's appetite for electric stimulation in some brain regions increases as hunger increases: the animal will respond much faster when hungry than when full. We are performing similar tests in other places in the brain with variations of thirst and sex hormones. We have already found that there are areas where the rewarding effects of a brain stimulus can be abolished by castration and restored by injections of testosterone.

Our present tentative conclusion is that emotional and motivational mechanisms can indeed be localized in the brain; that certain portions of the brain are sensitive to each of the basic drives.

Scientific American, 1956.

1. *Comprehension*

Read this text carefully, making notes about the information requested below:

	Paragraph
– the electrodes, their stimulating tips	*1*
– the testing	
– electrodes in the sensory and motor systems	*2*
– electrodes in the mid—line system	
– electrodes in the lower part of the mid—line system	
– the author's tentative explanation of this	
– stimulation of the hypothalamus	*3*
– stimulation of the rhinencephalon	
– both stimulation rates	
– the animals' preferences between stimulation and food. Examples	*4*
– the working hypothesis	*5*
– hunger and stimulation	*6*
– castration and testosterone	
– conclusion	*7*

2. *Writing*

Without any further reference to the text, write a summary of it from your notes.

3. *Activity*

Discussion. Are similar experiments still being carried out?
What is your opinion of their utility?

Text C

The Split Brain

Michael Gazzaniga, 1967

The physiologist Roger Sperry was interested in the function of the "corpus callosum" and undertook a programme of research (first with Myers, using rats and *later with Gazzaniga, with human patients). The "corpus callosum" *is an enormous band of white substance (therefore, axons) which is situated in the middle of the brain. If the "corpus callosum" of the cat is surgically sectioned down its length, it causes the animal no apparent suffering but its left side can to longer distinguish the actions of its right side. The "corpus callosum" is therefore a kind of cable that ensures communication between the two cerebral hemispheres. Occasionally (following lesions, operations caused by a tumour or an epileptic zone) there is partial or total section of the "corpus callosum". Can we then talk with a split brain?*

1. Visual input to *bisected brain** was limited to one hemisphere by presenting information only in one visual field. The right and left fields of view are projected, via the *optic chiasm**, to the left and right hemispheres of the brain respectively. If a person fixes his gaze on a point, therefore, information to the left of the point goes only to the right hemisphere and information to the right of the point goes to the left hemisphere. Stimuli in the left visual field cannot be described by a *split-brain** patient because of the disconnection between the right hemisphere and the *speech center**, which is in the left hemisphere.

What devices were used for the tests?

2. We come now to the main question on which we centered our studies, namely how the separation of the hemispheres affects the mental capacities of the human brain. For these psychological tests we used two different *devices**. One was visual: a picture or written information was flashed (for a *tenth of a second**) in either the right or the left visual field, so that the information was transmitted only to the left or to the right brain hemisphere. The other type of test was tactile: an object was placed out of view in the patient's right or left hand, again for the purpose of conveying the information to just one hemisphere—the hemisphere on the side opposite the hand.

What was the reaction of patients presented with "left-hemisphere" information?

3. When the information (visual or tactile) was presented to the dominant left hemisphere, the patients were able to deal with and describe it quite normally, both orally and in writing. For example, when a picture of a spoon was shown in the right visual field or a spoon was placed in the right hand, all the patients readily identified and described it. They were able to read out written messages and to perform problems in calculation that were presented to the left hemisphere.

What were the differences with "right-hemisphere" information?
In the author's view, what made the patients guess at the identity of the objects?

4. In contrast, when the same information was presented to the right hemisphere, it failed to elicit such spoken or written responses. A picture transmitted to the right hemisphere evoked either a *haphazard guess** or no verbal response at all. Similarly, a pencil placed in the left hand (behind a screen that cut off vision) might be called a can opener or a cigarette lighter, or the patient might not even attempt to describe it. The *verbal guesses** presumably came not from the right hemisphere but from the left, which had no perception of the object but might attempt to identify it from indirect clues.

The author suggests that, in the bisected

5. Did this impotence of the right hemisphere mean that its surgical separation from the left had reduced its mental powers

brain, the right hemisphere is :
❑ *the accuracy in its discernment with most patients*
❑ *totally impotent in all patients*
❑ *sometimes capable of discerning tactile information.*
Is there any indication that bisected brain patients were capable of "tactile reasoning"? If so, what? Could these same patients proceed to "verbal reasoning"?

to an imbecilic level? The earlier tests of its nonverbal capacities suggested that this was almost certainly not so. Indeed, when we switched to asking for nonverbal answers to the visual and tactile information presented in our new psychological tests, the right hemisphere in several patients showed considerable capacity for accurate performance. For example, when a picture of a spoon was presented to the right hemisphere, the patients were able to feel around with the left hand among a varied group of objects (screened from sight) and select a spoon as a match for the picture. Furthermore, when they were shown a picture of a cigarette they succeeded in selecting an ashtray, from a group of 10 objects that did not include a cigarette, as the article most closely related to the picture. Oddly enough, however, even after their correct response, and while they were holding the spoon or the ashtray in their left hand, they were unable to name or describe the object or the picture. Evidently the left hemisphere was completely *divorced, in perception and knowledge**, from the right.

To what extent could patients recognize visual stimuli?

6. Other tests showed that the right hemisphere did possess a certain amount of language comprehension. For example, when the word "pencil" was flashed to the right hemisphere, the patients were able to pick out a pencil from a group of unseen objects with the left hand. And when a patient held an object in the left hand (out of view), although he could not say its name or describe it, he was later able to point to a card on which the name of the object was written.

Scientific American, 1967

1. *Comprehension*

Read the first paragraph of the text then fill in this diagram:

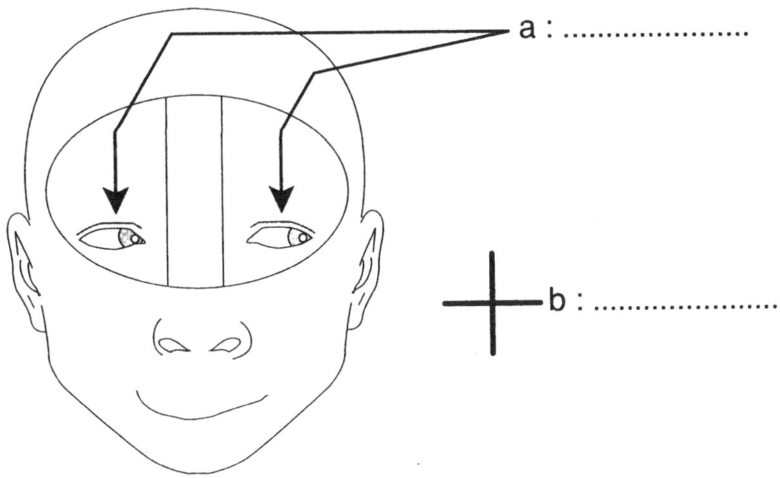

Can he tell you what he is looking at?

2. *Vocabulary*

Re—read the text now. Do you know the meanings of the following?

Para 3: spoon
Para 4: to elicit
Para 4: can-opener
Para 5: match
Para 5: ashtray

Text D

"Our instincts revealed in the aquarium"

Niko Tinbergen, 1952 (Nobel Prize 1973)

Are our behavior patterns instinctive or acquired? Patient study of animals in their natural habitat has cast an extraordinary light on this subject. Three Nobel Prize-winners have contributed to this research: Konrad Lorenz, best known for his work on aggressivity; Karl van Frisch, for his studies on the language of bees and Tinbergen, for his research on stickleback, a small freshwater fish whose behavior is rich in information about the hidden mechanisms of motivation.

(Do exercises 1 and 2 before reading the text)

1. When I was a young lecturer in zoology at the University of Leyden 20 years ago, I was asked to organize a laboratory course in animal behavior for undergraduates. In my quest for animals that could be used for such a purpose, I remembered the sticklebacks I had been accustomed as a boy to catch in the ditches near my home and to raise in a backyard aquarium. It seemed that they might be ideal laboratory animals. They could be hauled in numbers out of almost every ditch; they were tame and hardy and small enough to thrive in a tank no larger than a hatbox.

What were the advantages of the stickleback for the author's experiments? What other animals has the author worked with?

2. I soon discovered that in choosing these former pets I had struck oil. They are so tame that they submit unfrightened to laboratory experiments, for the stickleback, like the hedgehog, depends on its spines for protection and is little disturbed by handling. Furthermore, the stickleback turned out to be an excellent subject for studying innate behavior, which it displays in some remarkably dramatic and intriguing ways. We found it to be the most reliable of various experimental animals that we

worked with (including newts, bees, water insects and birds), and it became the focus of a program of research in which we now use hundreds of sticklebacks each year. The stickleback today is also a popular subject in various other zoological laboratories in Europe, notably at the universities in Groningen and Oxford. To us this little fish is what the rat is to many American psychologists.

How can study of the behaviour of stickleback give us information on human behaviour?

3. To get light on the behavior of man, particulary his *innate drives** and conflicts, it is often helpful to study the elements of behavior in a simple animal. Here is a little fish that exhibits a complicated pattern of activities, all dependent on *simple stimuli and drives**. We have studied and analyzed its behavior by a large number of experiments, and have learned a good deal about why the stickleback behaves as it does.

What is the significance of the colour red?
The author quotes an extreme example of "colour provocation". What is it?
How did the author verify this provocation?

4. Let us begin with the stimulus that causes one stickleback to attack another. Early in our work we noticed that a male patrolling its territory would attack a red-colored intruder much more aggressively than a fish of some other color. Even a red mail van passing our windows at a distance of 100 yards could make the males in the tank charge its glass side in that direction. To investigate the reactions to colors we made a number of *rough models** of sticklebacks and painted some of the dummies red, some pale silver, some green. We rigged them up on thin wires and presented them one by one to the males in the tank. We found that the red models were always more provoking than the others, though even the silvery or green intruders caused some hostility.

What other tests were performed?

5. In much the same way we tested the influence of shape, size, type of body movement and other stimuli, relating them to specific behavior in nest building, courting, attack, zigzag, fanning and so on. We discovered, for example, that a male swollen with food was courted as if it were a female.

What does the author say about the discernment of the female stickleback when confronted with red?
What are his conclusions?
What have the mail truck, the snout and the glass rod in common?

6. As our work proceeded, we saw that the effective stimuli differed from one reaction to another, even when two reactions were caused by the same object. Thus a female will follow a red model wherever it leads; she will even make frantic efforts to enter a non-existent nest wherever the model is poked into the sand. Once she is in a real nest, she can be induced to spawn merely by prodding the base of her tail with a glass rod, even after she has seen the red fish that led her there removed. At one moment the male must give the visual signal of red; at the next, this stimulus is of no importance and only the tactile sensation counts. This observation led us to conclude that the stickleback responds simply to "sign stimuli", i.e., to a few characteristics of an object rather than to the object as a whole. A red fish or a red mail truck, a thrusting snout or a glass rod—it is the signal, not the object, that counts. A similar dependence on sign stimuli, which indicates the existence of special central nervous mechanisms, has been found in other species. It seems to be typical of innate behavior, and many social relationships in animals apparently are based on a system of signs.

Scientific American, 1952

1. *Pre-reading activity*

Many children fish for "tiddlers", that is, small fish no more than an inch long that can be caught often enough without using a hook. The unfortunate garden worm or rolled bread is usually the best bait.
Did you ever go fishing as a child? What do you remember about your experiences?

2. *Comprehension*

The first paragraph of this text refers to the author's childhood memories, which have a certain charm.
Before reading it, try to match the following:

A. quest	1. a sort of small lake
B. ditch	2. non-aggressive
C. tame	3. strong, adaptable
D. hardy	4. search

A	B	C	D

- "to thrive" means "to live fully, to prosper"
- "to haul" means "to take out, to extract" (in this context)

Now read *paragraph 1*
Why did the author choose sticklebacks for his experiments?

3. *Vocabulary*

Now read the text again, guessing the following words/expressions from their contexts:

Para 2:
- to strike oil
- hedgehog
- to handle
- newts
- bees

Para 4:
- mail van
- dummies
- to rig something up

Para 5:
- to court
- fanning
- swollen

Para 6:
- to poke
- to spawn
- to prod
- snout

4. *Between the lines*

How would you describe the tone of the last sentence of paragraph 2?

Lexique

Acetylcholine : acétylcholine

L'un des "grands neurotransmetteurs" et qui déclenche entre autre l'activité du muscle.

Adrenal glands : glandes surrénales (au-dessus des reins) et qui secrètent l'adrénaline.

Avoidance effect : évitement (l'animal fuit ou attaque)

Axon terminal : terminal de l'axone

L'axone se termine par des petits bourrelets qui contiennent des vésicules contenant les neurotransmetteurs.

Bar-presses per hour : fréquence d'appuis par heure

Le comportement mesuré dans la boite de Skinner est le nombre d'appuis sur une barre par le rat.

(To) bind : se lier (relier)

L'image de la clé dans la serrure (ou d'une carte magnétique) permet de se représenter le "lien" d'un neurotransmetteur sur le récepteur (un radical chimique) de la protéine qui sert de canal. La clé ouvre le canal ionique de la protéine qui fonctionne alors comme une vanne ouverte.

Bisected brain : cerveau séparé

Blood-brain barrier : barrière hémato-méningée (ou méningée)

Les méninges qui entourent le cerveau servent en partie à le protéger notamment en servant de "filtre" : la barrière hémato-méningée.

Brain stem : tronc cérébral

Catecholamines : catécholamines

Neurotransmetteurs de la même famille chimique, noradrénaline et dopamine.

Caudate nucleus : noyau caudé

Fait partie des centres cérébraux du mouvement.

Cell bodies : corps cellulaires (des neurones, les axones étant leur prolongement)

Cerebellum : cervelet

Cerebral cortex : cortex cérébral

Chemically-gated : à ouverture chimique

Chlorpromazine : chlorpromazine

Célèbre neuroleptique : médicament qui a permis un soulagement de nombreuses maladies mentales de types psychoses, notamment dans les phases maniaques (excitation) ; elle agirait par un blocage des systèmes à dopamine.

Chronic activation : activation chronique, ou régulière

Corpus Callosum : corps calleux

"Darting" : fléchette-seringue (tiré par un fusil destiné à anesthésier les animaux sauvages à distance : cf. votre documentaire animalier habituel)

Devices : plans d'expérience

Divorced, in perception and knowledge : divorcé pour la perception et la connaissance

Sans les corps calleux, chaque hémisphère ne "sait" pas ce que perçoit ou fait l'autre.

Drugs : médicaments (drogues bénéfiques ou "maléfiques" en américain)

Free-ranging baboons : babouins librement hiérarchisés

Les babouins comme la plupart des singes vivent dans une colonie très hiérarchisée avec des mâles dominants et d'autres, dominés ou soumis.

Gating mechanism : mécanisme de vanne (ou d'écluse)

Les vannes s'ouvrent ou se ferment en fonction de deux sortes d'événements (cf. texte).

Haphazard guess : devinement au hasard

Hypothalamus : hypothalamus

L'"ordinateur" de la vie végétative ; certains secteurs sont spécialisés dans les grands systèmes motivationnels et végétatifs, faim, soif, sexe, vomissement, lactation, ovulation...

Innate drives : besoins innés

Littéralement "mobiles" innés ; le terme "mobile" (drive) est une concession à la terminologie behavioriste (introduit par Clark Hull) ; par la suite Tinbergen proposera son propre vocabulaire notamment les IRM (Innate Releasing Mechanisms) c'est-à-dire les mécanismes innés de déclenchement.

Ionic channels : canaux ioniques

L'axone peut être comparé à un canal avec ses rives, la membrane, et de loin en loin des vannes (ou écluses) : les canaux ioniques. Les vannes communiquent avec l'extérieur (comme un canal qui s'alimente dans un lac) sur le milieu fluide dans lequel baignent les cellules.

Ion pump : pompe ionique

Lorsque le canal ionique (la vanne) est ouvert, un "flot" d'ions sodiums se déversent à l'intérieur de l'axone, augmentant le potentiel électrique positif (puisque les ions sodium sont positifs). Pour rétablir l'équilibre, d'autres vannes s'ouvrent et rejettent des ions potassium (positifs également) à l'extérieur. Ce dispositif fonctionne comme une pompe.

Locus ceruleus : locus ceruleus

De nombreuses structures cérébrales ont un nom anatomique latin ; "usine" à Noradrénaline, située à la base du cerveau.

Luteinizing hormone-releasing hormone : hormone de l'hormone lutéine de déclenchement.

Il s'agit d'une triple cascade, de l'hypothalamus à l'hypophyse et enfin à la glande endocrine terminale. Lutéine, qui signifie en latin "jaune", vient de ce qu'une glande sexuelle (femelle) est appelée "corps jaune" à cause de sa couleur apparente.

Mid-line system : partie médiane du cerveau

Monoamine oxidase inhibitors : Inhibiteurs de la Monoamine oxydase (IMAO)

Certaines dépressions sont dues à une chute de neurotransmetteurs "excitants" comme les amines (noradrénaline). Comme un mécanisme synaptique normal est la diffusion d'enzymes qui mangent le trop plein de ces amines (les Inhibiteurs), les pharmacologues ont fabriqué des "mangeurs" de ces inhibiteurs ce qui relève le taux des amines : les IMAO s'avèrent être des puissants antidépresseurs.

Mood elevation : élévation de l'humeur, excitation

Nerve impulse : influx nerveux

Le concept est utilisé ici comme un terme familier sans référence à l'ancien modèle du courant électrique.

Optic chiasma : chiasma optique

Les deux nerfs optiques se croisent et ce croisement s'appelle "chiasma" ; le trajet est complexe mais le champ visuel droit est analysé par l'hémisphère gauche et inversement. Il y a également inversion pour la motricité.

Parkinsonism : Maladie de Parkinson

Caractérisée par un manque de contrôle des mouvements, tremblements, etc (atteinte du noyau caudé)

Parkinson-like tremor : tremblement de type (like) Parkinson

Pituitary gland : hypophyse

Glande à la base du cerveau reliée par sa partie supérieure (de nature nerveuse) à l'hypothalamus et déclenchant dans sa partie inférieure (de nature endocrinienne) les hormones qui elles-mêmes vont activer les glandes endocrines de l'organisme, en particulier, dans le texte, la testostérone dans les testicules.

"Pleasure" centers : centres du plaisir

Plummet : chuter, dégringoler (littéralement tomber comme un plomb)

Pore : pore (trou)

La membrane, très mince contient de loin en loin des pores qui sont des protéines plus grosses en forme de canal, et qui laissent passer les ions : ce sont les canaux ioniques, les vannes.

Precursor : précurseur

Molécule ou substance chimique dont la transformation (par des enzymes) permet la fabrication du neurotransmetteur par le corps humain.

Punishing effect : punition (ou renforcement négatif)

Recorded automatically : enregistrées (les réponses) automatiquement

La boîte de Skinner permet un enregistrement automatique, sans effet perturbateur de l'expérimentateur.

Resting state : potentiel de repos

Lorsqu'aucune activité électrique ou moléculaire ne trouble l'activité normale de la cellule nerveuse.

Rewarding effect : récompense (ou renforcement positif)

La technique comportementale utilisée est celle du conditionnement opérant dans une boite de Skinner ; celle-ci est une sorte de distributeur automatique pour rat où un appui sur une barre déclenche la chute d'une boulette de nourriture (récompense ou renforcement positif). Dans la technique de Olds, le renforcement habituel est remplacé par un renforcement intra-cérébral (une stimulation dans une zone qui fait "plaisir").

Rhinencephalon : rhinencéphale (ou cerveau olfactif)

Système complexe du cerveau autour des noyaux olfactifs (d'où le nom de cerveau olfactif). Appelé aussi "système limbique", il est au centre des comportements motivationnels et émotionnels.

Rough models : modèles approximatifs

Plus tard, appelés "leurres" (decoys)

Simple stimuli : stimulus simples

Concession au Behaviorisme : stimulus sera remplacé plus tard par "stimulus signaux" ou simplement "signaux".

Sites : sites (de réception)

Les lieux de la synapse (ou plus globalement des structures cérébrales) où se fixe ce neurotransmetteur.

Split-brain : cerveau dédoublé

Speech center : centre du langage

Les systèmes du langage sont généralement dans l'hémisphère gauche. Des recherches récentes notamment sur des sujets asiatiques précisent que l'hémisphère gauche n'est spécialisé que pour le langage phonétique (les langages pictographiques seraient dominants dans l'hémisphère droit, et les dessins ainsi que la compréhension dans les deux hémisphères).

Stress : état de choc ; choc (ou tension, surtension) mais le terme franglais "stress" semble irrévocablement implanté en tant que concept technique.

Certains y voient un synonyme d'"émotion" mais "émotion" est plutôt réservé pour des états spécifiques, colère, peur, alors que le stress est non spécifique.

Subordinate : dominés ou soumis

Substancia nigra : substance noire

Partie de la base du cerveau qui est "l'usine" à dopamine.

Synapses : synapse

La synapse est le lieu de jonction entre deux neurones.

Tenth of a second : 1/10e de seconde (ou 100 millisecondes)

Pour étudier un hémisphère, on présente un stimulus visuel (objet ou mot) dans le champ visuel opposé. Mais sachant que les yeux bougent, il faut que la présentation soit très rapide pour éviter que l'objet soit vu dans un autre champ visuel. On estime que 1/10e de seconde est suffisant pour empêcher une saccade oculaire.

Trigger : déclencher

Verbal guess : devinement verbal (d'après des indices indirects)

Voltage-gated : à ouverture électrique

Part 8

Statistical methods and Computational Sciences

1

"What are Statistics for?"

George Snedecor and William Cochran, 1968

This text, written by two well-known statisticians is a definition of what statistics are and how they can be used. Snedecor is associated with the famous F (of Snedecor) in the analysis of variance while Cochran (with Cox) has defined several experimental plans which have since become classics.

(Do exercises 1 and 2 before reading the text)

How do most statistical investigators work?

1. The subject matter of the field of statistics has been described in various ways. According to one definition, statistics deals with techniques for collecting, analyzing, and drawing conclusions from data. This description helps to explain why an introduction to statistical methods is useful to students who are preparing themselves for a career in one of the sciences and to persons working in any branch of knowledge in which much quantitative research is largely concerned with gathering and *summarizing** observations or measurements made by *planned experiments**, by *questionnaire surveys**, by the records of a sample of cases of a particular kind, or by combing past published work on some problem. From these summaries, the *investigator** draws conclusions that he hopes will have broad validity.

Say how similar work methods help gather necessary agricultural, industrial or political information

2. The same intellectual activity is involved in much other work of importance. Samples are extensively used in keeping a continuous watch on the output of production lines in industry, in obtaining national and regional estimates of crop yields and of business and employment conditions, in the auditing of financial statements, in checking for the possible adulteration of foods, in gauging public opinion and voter preferences, in learning how well the public is informed on current issues, and so on.

The author states that statistics have no "magic formula" for interpreting information, but how does he qualify this statement?

3. Acquaintance with the main ideas in statistical methodology is also an appropriate part of a general education. In newspapers, books, television, radio, and speeches we are all continuously exposed to statements that draw general conclusions: for instance, that the cost of living rose by 0.3% in the last month, that smoking of cigarettes is injurious to health, that users of "Blank's" toothpaste have 23% fewer cavities, that a television program had 18.6 million viewers. When an *inference**

of this kind is of interest to us, it is helpful to be able to form our own judgment about the truth of the statement. Statistics has no magic formula for doing this in all situations, for much remains to be learned about the problem of making sound inferences. But the basic ideas in statistics assist us in thinking clearly about the problem, provide some guidance about the conditions that must be satisfied if sound inferences are to be made, and enable us to detect many inferences that have no good logical foundation.

How can the statistician be sure that the "sample" represents the "aggregate"?

4. A sample consists of a small collection from some larger aggregate about which we wish information. The sample is examined and the facts about it learned. Based on these facts, the problem is to make correct inferences, about the aggregate or population. It is the sample what we observe, but it is the population which we seek to know.

What does the author mean by "variation"?

5. This would be no problem were it not for ever-present variation. If all individuals were alike, a sample consisting of a single one would give complete information about the population. Fortunately, there is endless variety among individuals as well as their environments. A consequence is that successive samples are usually different. Clearly, the facts observed in a sample cannot be taken as facts about the population. Our job then is to reach appropriate conclusions about the population despite sampling variation.

Sampling problems can be exacerbated when dealing with cold mice or one's friends. How?

6. But not every sample contains information about the population sampled. Suppose the objective of an experimental sampling is to determine the growth rate in a population of young mice fed a new diet. Ten of the animals are put in a cage for the experiment. But the cage gets located in a cold draught or in a dark corner. Or an unnoticed infection spreads among the mice in the cage. If such things happen, the growth rate in the sample may give no worthwhile information about that in the population of normal mice. Again, suppose an interviewer in an opinion poll picks only families among his friends whom he thinks it will be pleasant to visit. His sample may not at all represent the opinions of the population. This brings us to a second problem: to collect the sample in such a way that the sought-for information is contained in it.

The investigator is confronted with two problems. What are they?

7. So we are confronted with the twin problems of the investigator: to design and conduct his sampling so that it shall be representative of the population; then, having studied the sample, to make correct inferences about the sampled population.

What does the author mean by "differences"?

What are "treatments"?

8. Investigations are often designed to discover and evaluate differences between effects rather than the effects themselves. It is the difference between the amounts learned under two methods of teaching, the difference between the degrees of relief reported from two pain-relieving drugs that is wanted. In this chapter we consider the simplest investigation of this type, in which two groups or two procedures are compared. In experimentation, these procedures are often called the treatments. Such a study may be conducted in two ways.

What is involved in "paired sampling"?
What role does "heavy exercise" have in "self-pairing"?

9. Paired samples. Pairs of similar individuals or things are selected. One treatment is applied to one member of each pair, the other treatment to the second member. The members of a pair may be two students of similar ability; two patients of the same age and sex who have just undergone the same type of operation; or two male mice from the same litter. A common application occurs in self-pairing in which a single individual is measured on two occasions. For example, the blood pressure of a subject might be measured before and after heavy exercise. For any pair, the difference between the measurements given by the two members is an estimate of the difference in the effects of the two treatments or procedures.

10. With only a single pair it is impossible to say whether the difference in behavior is to be attributed to the difference in treatment, to the natural variability of the individuals, or partly to both. There must be a number of pairs. The data to be analyzed consist of a sample of differences in measurement.

What is "independent sampling" and in what circumstances is it most used?

11. Independent samples. This case, which is commoner, arises whenever we wish to compare the means of two populations and have drawn a sample from each quite independently. We might have a sample of men aged 50-55 and one of men aged 30-35, in order to compare the amounts spent on life insurance. Or we might have a sample of high school seniors from rural schools and one from urban schools, in order to compare their knowledge of current affairs as judged by a special examination on this subject. Independent samples are widely used in experimentation when no suitable basis for pairing exists, as, for example, in comparing the lengths of life of two types of drinking glass under the ordinary conditions of restaurant use.

The Iowa State University Press
Ames, Iowa, USA, 1968

Exercises 1

1. *Pre-reading activity*

Look at this statement:

"Only 37 % of the students passed the exam"

What does it mean? Rather, what can we deduce from the statement (assuming it is true)?

– that most of the students were lazy/unmotived/on holiday?
– that the exam was too difficult/badly constructed?
– or that it was a good result, bearing in mind that the exam is highly competitive?
In other words, the statement out of context says something but means very little.
What about this statement:

"Nine out of ten of the Express Method students spoke English perfectly after only 50 hours' tuition"

Make similar hypotheses about the validity of this statement.

Now, on to statistics.

2. *Vocabulary*

You may have a few difficulties with the following:

Para 1:	– subject matter	→	the "contents" of the subject
	– to gather	→	to collect
	– to comb	→	to search through (in this context)
Para 2:	– crop yields	→	the amount of crops (eg wheat, barley) harvested in a year
Para 8:	– glassware	→	objects made of glass or crystal
	– pain-relieving	→	aspirin is a pain-relieving drug
Para 9:	– litter	→	a group noun : the new-born young of many mammals
Para 11:	– quite	→	totally (in the context)

3. *Grammar review*

• The First Conditional (reviewed) and the Second Conditional. Their differences.

Look at these two sentences:

– ⓐ *"I'll write to her if I have time"*
– ⓑ *"I'd write to her if I had time"*

In sentence ⓐ the condition is "open"; there is no suggestion of doubt or uncertainty.
In sentence ⓑ however, there is a definite suggestion that "It is unlikely, if not impossible that I will write to her because I have no time/am too busy etc..."
The sentence ⓑ types are called "hypothetical conditionals" and are formed as follows:

PERSON + MODAL VERB + INFINITIVE – CONDITION WORD
– + PERSON + PAST

a) Here are some hypothetical conditional sentences. Translate them into French:

- She'd learn to play the piano if she had enough money for the lessons
- If he won the election, he might lower taxes
- If they worked harder, they could get better exam results

b) Now fill in the appropriate condition form in the following sentences, choosing the verbs from the box

BE	COME	VOTE	STOP	MISS	RING	REDUCE

– In case he __________, I __________ in the kitchen
– If I __________ you, I __________ smoking
– I __________ delighted if she __________, but you know how she hates parties
– I __________ vote for him even if he __________ unemployment
– If her flight __________ late, she __________ the connection

(Sometimes either a negative or an affirmative response is possible. But be logical).

c) Make appropriate sentences from the notes below:

– She (visit) California	(save) enough money
– They (retire) to the Bahamas	(win) the Loto
– You (write) essays faster	(use) a word processor
– I (be) a teacher of psychics	(obtain) a better job
– She (able to travel) so freely	(be) married

d) Look at the text:

Para 5. Sentence 2: an example of a hypothetical conditional
Para 6. Sentence 6: an example of an open conditional with "may"

4. *Between the lines*

This fairly technical text is rendered more approachable by use of exemplification (see *Para 3*). Find other examples of this in the text.

5. *Activity*

a) Take the horoscope columns from at least four different popular newspapers, then number these papers 1 to 4 (or 5). Taking newspaper 1 as an arbitrary reference, draw a similar table to the one below and state (Yes/No) if the predictions of each paper are roughly the same as the reference paper or not.

Newspapers	1	2	3	4	5
ARIES					
TAURUS					
GEMINI					
CANCER					
LEO					
VIRGO					
LIBRA					
SCORPIO					
SAGITTARIUS					
CAPRICORN					
AQUARIUS					
PISCES					
TOTAL					
%					

After that, make statistics: count one point for Yes (in a group, decide by majority vote) and compute the total and the percentage of successes (or concordance).

From this activity, do you conclude that astrology is a science or a game?

b) Information-exchange

In sub-groups of three or four, discuss and choose one subject about which you will conduct a survey on your colleagues. It could be (for example):

- eating or drinking habits
- study habits
- education and upbringing etc...

Now decide on ten questions to be asked about your chosen subject and make a check list on which you will note replies.

Now circulate among your colleagues (from different sub-groups) asking your questions, noting responses and answering their questions (3 or 4 interviews each).
Re-form into your original sub-group. You should have information about at least ten colleagues by now.
Prepare a statistical presentation of this information, using percentages, fractions, ratios etc. (eg "40%/nearly a half/2:5 of the sample were educated privately/work to pay for their studies" etc.)
Now present your findings, drawing conclusions where possible.

Do your conclusions have "broad validity"? (cf *Para* 1 of the text)

2

Vision by Man and Machine

Tomaso Poggio, 1984

The author explains clearly how perspectives for the future of information processing cannot be simplistically imagined by equating the function of neurons with transistors. Following the orientation of Wiener and others in the theory of information, the brain and the computer are particular cases of systems capable of processing information. Their functional resemblances, however, can help us to form hypotheses about their mechanisms.

1. The development of computers of increasing power and sophistication often stimulates comparisons between them and the human brain, and these comparisons are becoming more earnest as computers are applied more and more to tasks formerly associated with essentially human activities and capabilities. Indeed, it is widely expected that a coming generation of computers and robots will have sensory, motor and even "intellectual" skills closely resembling our own. How might such machines be designed? Can our rapidly growing knowledge of the human brain be a guide? And at the same time can our advances in "artificial intelligence" help us to understand the brain?

2. At the level of their *hardware* * (the brain's or a computer's) the differences are great. The neurons, or nerve cells, in a brain are small, delicate structures bound by a complex membrane and closely packed in a medium of supporting cells that control a complex and probably quite variable chemical environment. They are very unlike the wires and etched crystals of semiconducting materials on which computers are based. In the organization of the hardware the differences also are great.

3. How, then, are brains and computers alike? Clearly there must be a level at which any two mechanisms can be compared. One can compare the tasks they do. "To bring the good news from Ghent to Aix" is a description of a task that can be done by satellite, telegraph, horseback messenger or pigeon post equally well (unless other constraints such as time are specified). If, therefore, we assert that brains and computers function as *information-processing systems* *, we can develop descriptions of the tasks they perform that will be equally applicable to either. We shall have a common language in which to discuss them: the language of information processing. Note that in this language descriptions of tasks are decoupled from descriptions of the hardware that perform them. This separability is at the foundation of the science of artificial intelligence.

Why is the faculty of vision vital for the creation of robots?

4. In no field have the descriptions of information-processing tasks been more precisely formulated than in the study of vision. On the one hand it is the dominant sensory modality of human beings. If we want to create robots capable of performing complex manipulative tasks in a changing environment, we must surely endow them with adequate visual powers.

Why has the author concentrated on stereopsis?

5. I shall concentrate on a particular aspect of the task, namely stereopsis, or stereo vision. Not the least of my reasons is the central role stereopsis has played in the work on vision that my colleagues and I have done at the Artificial Intelligence Laboratory of the Massachusetts Institute of Technology. In particular, stereopsis has simulated a close investigation of the very first steps in visual information processing.

What causes the phenomenon of stereopsis?

Why will neighbouring points in the visual field differ in their projections to the retina from the fixated point?

6. Stereopsis arises from the fact that our two eyes view the visual world from slightly different angles. To put it another way, the eyes converge slightly, so that their axes of vision meet at a point in the visual world. The point is said to be fixated by the eyes, that is, the image of the point falls on the center of vision of each retina. Any neighboring point in the visual field will then project to a point on each retina some distance from the center of vision. In general this distance will not be the same for both eyes. In fact, the disparity in distance will vary with the depth of the point in the visual field with respect to the fixated point.

How is stereopsis defined?

7. Stereopsis, then, is the decoding of three-dimensionality from binocular disparities. It might appear at first to be a straightforward problem in trigonometry. One might therefore be tempted to program a computer to solve it that way. The effort would fail.

Why can't photoreceptors in each eye receive the same image from a patch?

8. A group of contiguous photoreceptor in one eye can be thought of as looking along a line of sight to a patch of the surface of some object. The photoreceptors looking at the same patch of surface from the opposite eye must then be identified. Because of binocular disparity they will not be able at the same position with respect to the center of vision.

9. This, of course, is where the difficulty lies. For us the visual world contains surfaces that seem effectively labeled because they belong to distinct shapes in specific spatial relations to one another.

How did Julesz devise random-dot stereograms?

What were his findings?

10. A discovery made at AT&T Bell Laboratories by Bela Julesz (now at Rutgers University) shows the full extent of the problem. Julesz devised pairs of what he called random-dot stereograms. They are visual stimuli that contain no perceptual clues except binocular disparities. To make each pair he generated a random texture of black and white dots and made two copies of it. In one of the copies he shifted an area of the pattern, say a square. In the other copy he shifted the square in the opposite direction. He filled the resulting hole in each pattern with more random texture. Viewed one at a time each pattern looked uniformly random. Viewed through a stereoscope, so that each eye saw one of the patterns and the brain could fuse the two, the result was startling. The square gave a vivid impression of floating in front of its surroundings or behind them. Evidently stereopsis does not require the prior perception of objects or the recognition of shapes.

How does the author describe the "correspondence problem" and why is it important?

11. Julesz' discovery enables one to formulate the computational goal of stereopsis: it is the extraction of binocular disparities from a pair of images without the need for obvious monocular clues. In addition the discovery enables one to formulate the computational problem inherent in stereopsis. It is the correspondence problem: the matching of elements in the two images that correpond to the same location in space without the recognition of objects or their parts. In random-dot stereograms the black dots in each image are all the same: they have the same size, the same shape and the same brightness. Any one of them could in principle be matched with any one of a great number of dots in the other image. And yet the brain solves this false target dilemma: it consistently chooses only the correct set of matches.

If the brain can solve the "correspondence problem", what can we deduce about the brain?

12. It must use more than the dots themselves. In particular, the fact that the brain can solve the correspondence problem shows it exploits a set of implicit assumptions about the visual world, assumptions that constrain the correspondence problem, making it determined and solvable.

Scientific American, 1984.

Exercises 2

1. *Comprehension*

a) Read paragraphs 1 – 3 of the text, then choose the most accurate of the statements from those suggested below:

Para 1:
- ❏ As computers become more sophisticated, they are compared with the human brain.
- ❏ Increasingly, computers perform tasks hitherto associated with the human brain.
- ❏ Increasingly powerful computers can perform human activities.

Para 2: ❑ The hardware of the brain is different only in size from that of the computer.
❑ The hardware of the brain is different in size and organization from that of the computer.
❑ The hardware of the brain is different in sophistication from that of the computer.

Para 3: ❑ The brain processes information faster than the computer.
❑ Computers process information as fast as the brain
❑ Both process information.

b) What do you know about "bringing the good news from Ghent to Aix"? Now read the rest of the text, auswering the questions alongside.

2. *Vocabulary*

Match these words:

A. to endow — 1. surprising
B. straightforward — 2. to move, displace
C. a patch — 3. a large spot
D. to shift — 4. before
E. startling — 5. easy
F. prior — 6. to give

A	B	C	D	E	F

3. *Grammar review*

- **The genitive, or "where must I place the apostrophe?"**

Generally, apostrophes denoting possession are placed following the logic of the "possessor" rather than that of the "possessed".
Therefore, if the possessor is singular, we write:

"Mary Johnson's house"
"Mary Johnson's children" (the apostrophe before the s)

If the possessors are plural, we write:

"The Johnsons' house"
"The Johnsons' children" (the apostrophe after the s)

Note how the possessive of *irregular* plural nouns takes an apostrophe before the s:

"The child's toy"
"The children's toy (or toys)"

Note how, in certain *proper names*:

The car belonging to Mr James can be written as:
– either "Mr James' car"
– or "Mr James's car"
as "James" is a proper noun ending in s

Finally, note that in general we use the apostrophe genitive for living things. "The car's wheels" would sound unusual in most cases. "The wheels of the car" would be more common.

a) If and where necessary, make improvements and corrections to the following passage:

"The house's basic structure is sound but it's windows and the doors' frames need painting. The previous owners' children were badly-behaved and smashed the garage's windows. But you have a pleasant view over the fields and the village is only a few minutes walk away. There you'll find a butchers' shop, a pub and a post office."

b) Now look at paragraph 2 of the text, sentence 1. We can see that although "the brain" and "a computer" are not living things as such, they can take an apostrophe. (Otherwise the sentence would be unwieldy)

– Paragraph 11, sentence 1. "Julesz' discovery" does not take an s, though "Julesz's discovery" would have been perfectly acceptable.

4. *Between the lines*

Note how the author has achieved emphasis in *paragraph 4,* (sentence 1) and in *paragraph 5* (sentence 2)

Now write them as more neutral sentences.

5. *Translate into English*

Connaissances Déclaratives et Connaissances Procédurales

Une distinction fructueuse venue de l'Intelligence Artificielle (IA pour les initiés) concerne les connaissances déclaratives et procédurales. Un système expert (système intelligent de documentation) est composé à la fois d'une banque de données, la bibliothèque des informations de base, ce sont les connaissances déclaratives, et d'un générateur d'inférence qui produit les déductions non enregistrées en tant que telles, ce sont les connaissances procédurales. Cette distinction est très riche car elle permet d'expliquer qu'à partir d'un nombre fini d'informations stockées, on puisse fabriquer un nombre illimité d'énoncés. Ainsi, le langage permet de créer à partir d'un vocabulaire limité (même s'il comporte plusieurs dizaines de milliers de mots) un nombre illimité de récits à partir de moteurs d'inférence (logique) et syntaxique (les règles de grammaire). Un autre champ d'application est l'arithmétique cognitive : les recherches en psychologie chez l'enfant ou l'adulte ont ainsi montré que la table de multiplication était essentiellement de nature déclarative (cela change dans la mémoire des enfants avec l'introduction de la calculette électronique) tandis que la division et la soustraction sont de nature procédurale. Quant à l'addition, elle serait mixte comme l'est sans doute l'imagination fertile des créateurs...

6. *Activity*

a) Discussion. The hardware of the computer and the human brain are totally different, but both process information (*cf. paragraphs 2 and 3* of the text).

To what degree, and in what other fields of research (or other activity) can you envisage artificial intelligence replacing the human brain?

This could raise the problem of value-judgements. Do you agree that there is a "human domain" wherein artificial intelligence has no place? How would you define this domain?

Text A

Normal Distribution

Snedecor and Cochran, 1968

You can't go wrong with normal distribution. It's only normal...

What is the binomial curve?

Find some discrete and continuous variables

Why are mean and standards deviations so important in statistics?

1. De Moivre published its equation in 1733, twenty years after Bernoulli had given a comprehensive account of the *binomial**.

2. Indeed, De Moivre discovered the normal distribution when seeking an approximation to the binomial. The *discrete** variable has become *continuous** and the frequencies have merged into each other without a break.

3. This *normal distribution** is completely determined by two *constants** or *parameters**. First, there is the *mean**, μ, which locates the centers of the distribution. Second, the *standard deviation**, σ, measures the spread or variation of the individual measurements; in fact, σ is the *scale** (unit of measurement) of the variable which is normally distributed.

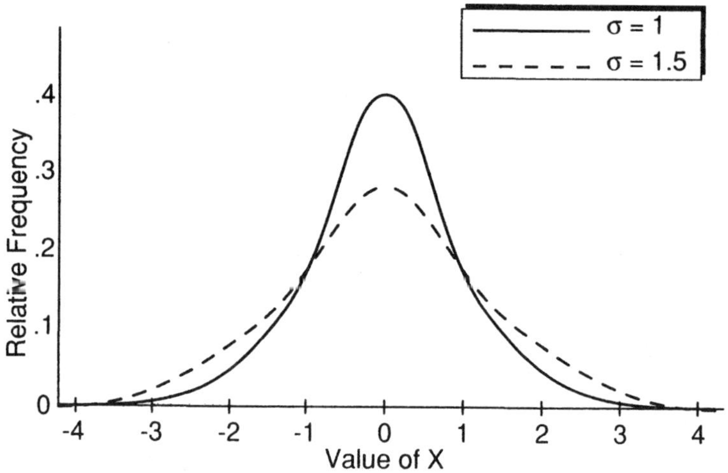

4. From the figure you see that within one *sigma** on either side of μ the frequency is decreasing ever more rapidly but beyond that point it decreases at a continuously lesser rate. By the time the variable, X, has reached $\pm 3\sigma$ the percentage frequencies are negligibly small. Theoretically, the frequency of occurrence never vanishes entirely, but it approaches zero as X increases indefinitely. The concentration of the measurements close to m is emphasized by the fact that over 2/3 of the observations lie in the interval $\mu \pm s$ while some 95% of them are in the interval $\mu \pm 2\sigma$. Beyond $\pm 3\sigma$ lies only 0.26% of the total frequency.

The *formula** for the ordinate or height of the normal curve is

$$y = \frac{1}{\sigma\sqrt{2\pi}} e^{-(X-\mu)^2 2\sigma^2}.$$

The Iowa State University Press, 1968.

1. *Discussion*

See Paragraph 4 – the theoretical consequences. Some people deny that genetic intelligence potential is distributed like a normal distribution. Imagine that intelligence was equally distributed from deficiency to genius (in a graph, this distribution would be called rectangular distribution). Draw two graphs. Which curve (normal or equivalent) would be predicted for the majority of average people?

2. *Activity*

In the class, find out about your colleagues' cigarette consumption in terms of cigarette units per student. Now, draw the corresponding distribution curve in a graph where the abciss is as below:

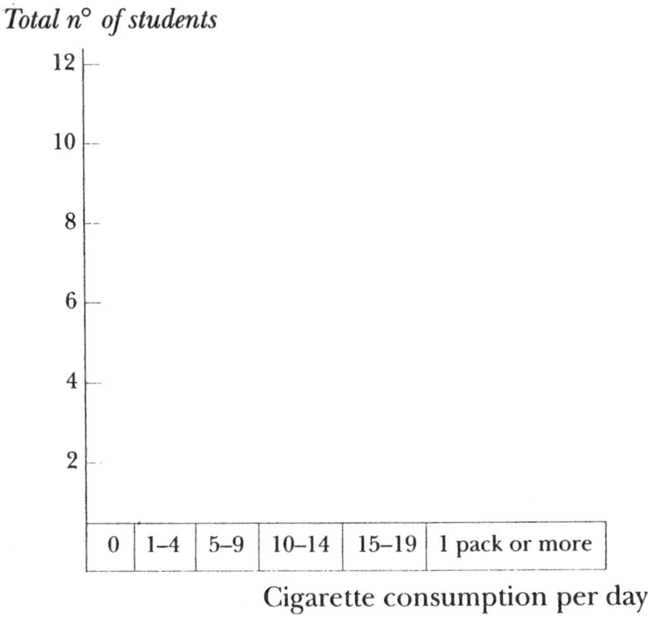

Find other variables for which you could easily construct a distribution curve (duration of sleep; the time you wake up; your height; the number of books you read per month, etc.)

Text B

Measurement of Correlation

Philip E. Vernon, 1965

The correlation or measure of resemblance between two series of marks or tests is a fundamental measure in psychology. With it, we can estimate resemblances between two school subjects, two tests or between age differences. Correlation is also a basic measure that allows us to make more sophisticated analyses such as a factorial analysis which shows up common denominators between several sets of tests or between human aptitudes. Vernon has done a lot of research into educational psychology and clearly explains an easily-calculable correlation cœfficient.

*Rank-order** *Correlation**.–A different method for determining correlations is available for data arranged in order, for example the orders of merit of a school class on two examinations. When the number of *cases** is greater than about 30, the figures involved become troublesomely big, but with a small number the method is much easier to use than the *product-moment method**. Often, therefore, sets of *scores** are turned into rank orders and the correlation between these orders is computed. The formula is as follows:

$$r = 1 - \frac{6\Sigma d^2}{N(N^2 - 1)}$$

where d is the difference between each person's two ranks. Such a correlation is often indicated by the Greek letter ρ *(rho)**, instead of by *r*.

Ex.–The second and third *columns** of the following *table** give the *marks** of eleven pupils on tests X_1 and X_2. The next two

Pupil	X_1	X_2	Ranks		*d*	d^2
A . .	65	75	6	4	2	4
B . .	85	66	1	7	6	36
C . .	64	58	7	9	2	4
D . .	78	82	3	1	2	4
E . .	60	58	8	9	1	1
F . .	70	80	5	$2\frac{1}{2}$	$2\frac{1}{2}$	6.25
G . .	83	80	2	$2\frac{1}{2}$	$\frac{1}{2}$	0.25
H . .	55	71	10	5	5	25
I . .	50	58	11	9	2	4
J . .	72	55	4	11	7	49
K . .	59	68	9	6	3	9
						142.5

columns show the ranks, pupil A being 6th on X_1, 4th on X_2, and so on. The *d* column gives the differences in rank, regardless of *sign**. These are *squared** and summed. Substituting in the formula:

$$r = 1 - \frac{6 \times 142.5}{11(121-1)} = 1 - 0.648 = +0.352$$

The measurement of Abilities University
of London Press, 1965

1. *Comprehension*

Look at this short text and table for one minute, answering the following questions:
a) What did the examinations seek to test?
b) How many examinations took place?
c) What is the maximum number of pupils that can be correlated in this way, and why?

Now look again:
What is r?
What is d?

2. *Activity*

Look carefully at the table and the resultant formula for the results of Pupil A.

Now take another pupil and, following the formula, work out his/her rank-order correlation.

Text C

The Psychology of Computers

Allan Collins and Ross Quillian, 1972

What do we call the interactive domain between computers and psychology? The term "cybernetics", invented by its founder Norbert Wiener (see Text 1: 2) was perfectly suitable for the study of machine and living systems. But the term has fallen out of use because of the interdisciplinary difficulties posed by its definition, which is a pity. The term "Artificial Intelligence" is elegant but too restrictive while "Cognitics" is far from restrictive but somewhat less than elegant. What about "Artificial Psychology"...?

(Do exercise 1 before readind the text).

When *computers** first set out to humble man, they thought it would be good fun to read, and talk, and answer questions. Well, by now they have gotten over their cockiness about reading and the like, though, in consequence, man has not gotten over his. Their failure was not for any lack of cleverness, though. Their basic mistake probably was in thinking they could skip over evolution, that their adeptness at artificial intelligence would let them fake their way past us in natural intelligence. Now, with humility written all over their inscrutable faces, computers are trying to revive their egos by imitating man.

One of the things computers missed out on in evolution is how to deal with similarity. They just never developed very good strategies for generalizing what they know about one situation to similar situations. Somehow, the simplest of organisms can do this, but computers do it only in ad hoc ways when they do it at all. Even the language ability that evolution worked so hard to produce appears to rely on this phylogenetically primative ability. Having missed out on evolution, the problem as computers see it is to take apart a language user without losing any pieces, to see if they can sort out how everything fits together. If they can do that, then they can pretend to read and talk just like people. Although their approach is dissembling, still, what is studied and artificial at first gradually becomes second nature.

When looked at from the point of view of computers instead of people, the problems of psychology appear quite different. Computers' interest in psychology stems from their desire to copy the way people think. They analyse people in terms of the way they themselves, at present, work: that is, in terms of strategies, routines and subroutines, *pointers**, lists, etc. In these terms, they feel they can imitate any kind of process from a chemical reaction to a confrontation between ego and id. It is not so important to them whether this is the best way to try to describe how different processes work, because it is the only kind of description that is of use to them. Put in philosophical terms, their approach is one of nominalism rather than realism.

In general, computers are more interested in the simple, straightforward human abilities rather than in *exotic phenomena** like perceptual illusions and *learning nonsense syllables**. This is because computers are, to a man, practical types. They want to walk before they try to run. So they focus on the common stuff of human existence like identifying what a figure is, comprehending what a sentence means, answering simple questions.

In organisation of Memory. Tulving and
Donaldson Academic Press, 1972

1. *Pre-reading activity*

Imagine you are an all-powerful computer and a mere human being is trying to program you to write a letter asking for a job. What mistakes will your programmer make?

2. *Comprehension*

- **Paragraph 1**

❑ Read the first paragraph of the text and answer the following TRUE/FALSE questions :

- Men still believe that computers can be made to read. (TRUE/FALSE)
- Computers are not clever. (TRUE/FALSE)
- Artificial intelligence replaces human intelligence. (TRUE/FALSE)
- Computers try to copy man. (TRUE/FALSE)

❑ Some of the vocabulary in this paragraph may cause problems

- "to humble" means "to humiliate", but what about these other verbs?

Try to guess them from the context.

- to get over something
- to skip over
- to fake

❑ Look at these nouns. What are their adjectives and what do they mean?

- cockiness
- cleverness
- adeptness

❑ The tone of this first paragraph is pleasantly light and amusing. Give some examples.

- **Paragraphs 2 – 4**

❑ Vocabulary notes:

Para 2: to miss out on → (in this context) to fail to understand
Para 4: the stuff of → the essence of

	Paragraphs
The authors state that computers cannot generalize. What example do they give? What conclusion do they draw?	*2*
What is the danger of computers in psychology?	*3*
According to the authors, the computer has severe limitations in psychology. What are they?	*4*

3. *Activity*

a) Text analysis. Obviously, Collins and Quillian have strong views about the "Psychology of Computers". Read through paragraphs 2 – 4, underlining the words/expressions used to make these views clear.

Classify them in terms of:

IRONY	DISPARAGEMENT
SLANG	HUMOUR

b) "Poor old machine", the authors seem to say about computers, "quick, accurate but limited."

Do you agree?

Lexique

Binomial : loi binomiale

Loi statistique courante de statistique qui correspond à une mesure discontinue (discrète). Par exemple, le total d'un questionnaire de dix questions oui/non pourra être indiqué en abcisse (l'axe horizontal) par les intervalles suivants : 0 oui, 1 oui, 2 oui, ... 5 oui... 8, 9 oui et 10 oui.

En général, on obtiendra une courbe (en escalier puisque l'axe n'est pas continu) avec un maximum de questionnaires où il y aura 5 oui, c'est la loi Binomiale.

Cases : cas (le nombre de cas, ou d'individus)

Columns : Colonnes du tableau et **Rows** = Rangées ou lignes du tableau

Computers : ordinateurs

Littéralement "calculateurs" ; les ordinateurs ont été effectivement dans leur prime enfance des calculateurs électroniques.

Constant : constante

Dans un souci de simplicité, les auteurs ne distinguent pas constante et paramètre, mais les constantes sont en principe invariables, comme π dans la formule de la loi normale qui est de façon constante égal à 3,14 et e = 2,71 (base des logarithmes naturels).

Continuous : continu

mesures continues, par exemple les notes de 0 à 20 ou des Quotients intellectuels de 40 à 140, etc.

Correlation : corrélation

Il existe plusieurs techniques de mesure de la corrélation que l'on appelle des coefficients de corrélation.

Discrete : discret ou discontinu : réponses oui ou non, + ou –, etc

Dotted curve : courbe en pointillé (en traits pointillés)

Exotic phenomena : phénomène exotique

Avec humour, les auteurs se moquent des psychologues classiques qui étudiaient les mécanismes mentaux à partir d'aberrations du fonctionnement en laissant de côté les phénomènes les plus courants, préfèrant l'analyse des illusions à celles des simples lettres de l'alphabet. Cependant dans d'autres domaines (voir texte 9 : 2) de la psychologie artificielle, comme la reconnaissance automatique, on essaie de rendre compte des phénomènes perceptifs y compris des aberrations comme les illusions perceptives.

Formula : formule

La formule ne doit pas effrayer l'étudiant en psychologie qui n'aura jamais à la calculer ; mais on voit par cette formule, que la loi normale (y) dépend (outre les deux constantes π et e dont la valeur est fixe une fois pour toute) de deux variables seulement, la moyenne (μ) et l'écart type (σ). En pratique, on ne se sert en statistiques que de la moyenne et de l'écart type.

Hardware : les composants (littéralement la "quincaillerie")

Par opposition, les programmes ont été dénommés "software" (= les logiciels).

Inference : inférence (prévision, généralisation)

Outre la Statistique Descriptive, il existe un second objectif des statistiques, la Statistique inférentielle (ou Tests statistiques) qui consiste à faire des prévisions à partir de l'échantillon testé (ex. une seule classe sur tout un collège). Des expériences et des calculs ont montré que la connaissance de la moyenne et de la variance (un indicateur de dispersion des mesures autour de la moyenne) permet d'estimer si le résultat trouvé dans l'échantillon peut être dû au hasard.

· **Information-processing system** : système de traitement de l'information

Investigator : expérimentateur

Learning nonsense syllables : apprentissage de syllabes sans signification

Voici un bon exemple de phénomène exotique. Les behavioristes ont eu l'illusion d'étudier l'apprentissage à partir de zéro en prenant des séquences de lettres au hasard, les syllabes sans signification, jusqu'à ce qu'on découvre que celles-ci sont apprises par assimilation à des mots ou des phrases. La technique des syllabes sans signification complique donc les mécanismes d'apprentissage plus qu'elle ne les simplifie...

Marks : notes (scolaires ; ici sur 100)

Les notes ou les corrélations sont fréquemment rangées dans un tableau (non cité dans le texte) avec les termes courants fréquents : "Columns" et "Rows"

Mean : moyenne, désignée par la lettre grecque μ (MU)

Mean est le terme technique, "average" qui signifie également "moyenne" a un sens plus courant.

Normal distribution : distribution normale

Quand on passe de mesures (sur l'axe des abcisses) discontinues (oui/non) à des mesures continues, la loi binomiale, en escalier, devient progressivement la loi normale.

Parameters : paramètres

Les paramètres (ou variables) varient, par exemple la note d'un élève.

Planned experiment : expérience planifiée ou plan d'expérience

L'expérimentation, pour vérifier des hypothèses, requiert des groupes de sujets (ou d'épreuves) affectés à des conditions. L'arrangement de ces groupes et conditions est le plan d'expérience.

Pointers : repères

Dans une liste d'instructions en informatique, on peut ajouter un repère qui renvoie à une autre instruction (par exemple dans le language basic GOTO : aller vers).

Product-moment method : méthode des moments composés

Une autre technique de corrélation basée sur les notes.

Questionnaire surveys : inventaire ou questionnaire

Dans certains domaines, psychologie sociale, personnalité, les recueils de mesures portent primitivement sur les réponses verbales des sujets, les questionnaires ou inventaires (ou listes à cocher : check lists).

Rank order : rang dans un classement (1er, 2ème, 3ème... dernier)

L'anglais Spearman a inventé le premier coefficient de corrélation basé sur les rangs des élèves (ou sujets en général) mais il existe d'autres coefficients basés sur la valeur des notes.

ρ**(rho)**

Le coefficient de Spearman est désigné par la lettre ρ tandis que le coefficient le plus commun (Bravais-Pearson) est désigné par la lettre r.

Scale : échelle (sous-entendu d'intervalles)

En statistique, on prend fréquemment l'écart type comme mesure standard d'intervalle entre les notes (ou les Quotients intellectuels) tout comme le centimètre ou les degrés Celsius dans d'autres phénomènes.

Scores : résultats ou scores

Sigma : lettre grecque qui désigne l'écart type : σ

Une autre mesure de la dispersion (non citée dans le texte mais que l'étudiant rencontrera) est le χ^2 (lettre grecque Chi que l'on prononce Ki) ou Chi Square, c'est-à-dire Chi au carré ou plus communément traduit en français par Chi deux.

Sign : signe (+ ou –)

Solid curve : courbe pleine (en trait plein)

Squared : au carré (élevé au carré)

Standard deviation : écart type

C'est un indicateur de l'écart des notes par rapport à la moyenne. Dans les tests statistiques, "standard deviation" signifie aussi écart standard (divisé par le nombre de mesures moins une : n–1)

Summarizing : résumer

Un objectif méconnu des statistiques chez les étudiants qui voient essentiellement dans les statistiques des méthodes compliquées, des formules et des calculs, c'est de résumer les données par quelques indices. Quoi de plus pratique qu'une moyenne ou un pourcentage par exemple, qui résume les totaux de 20 ou 300 (parfois plus) individus.

Ce premier objectif concerne la Statistique Descriptive.

Table (Matrix) : tableau ou matrice

On dit fréquemment matrice de corrélations pour un tableau de corrélations.

Appendix

Essentials for reading comprehension

If we assume that the non-native reader of specialist texts knows the basic structure and tenses of the English language, there are still at least three main areas that she/he often finds confusing. These are :

- link words (ie words or expressions which join ideas)
- compound nouns
- modal verbs (ie "defective" auxiliary verbs)

This appendix does not purport to be a definitive grammatical explanation of the above elements. Its aims are more limited — to provide a basic pathway through the traps. (Any reader interested in pursuing these matters further is directed to "A Communicative Grammar of English", by Leech & Svartvik).

Link words

There are many link words in English — "and" and "but" being the most common. It will help our understanding of these words if we group them into "families", each family representing a *NOTION*.
The most common notions to be found in texts are:

CONTRAST and *SIMILARITY*
CAUSE, EFFECT and *PURPOSE*
ADDITION

(A final notion, that of *FORECASTING,* is included in the "Modal Verbs" section of this appendix as a degree of probability).
We will explore each notion in turn. They have been grouped for the sake of clarity.

1. *Contrast and Similarity*

a) Contrast

Read the following sentences:

IT RAINED EVERY DAY. WE HAD A GOOD HOLIDAY.

How can we link these sentences to make a "logical" statement?
Obviously — "It rained every day <u>but</u> we had a good holiday."
The sentence is deliberately banal, but there are more sophisticated ways of implying contrast.
Read these sentences:

ALTHOUGH/THOUGH he worked hard, he failed the exam.

Funds were cancelled. *NEVERTHELESS/HOWEVER/YET,* she continued the research.

WHILE/WHILST/WHEREAS divorce statistics rose, couples continued to get married.

DESPITE/IN SPITE OF/NOTWITHSTANDING Freud's reputation, many of his theories are still bitterly disputed.

b) Similarity

We can express the notion of similarity in many ways.
Let's take a look at three fairly typical villages:

CLAYFORD	*OREFUL*	*ANGBRIDGE*
church	church	
pubs	pubs	pubs
no supermarket	no supermarket	no supermarket
cinema		
car park		car park

Now read these sentences describing these positive and negative similarities:

BOTH Clayford and Oreful have churches
ALL the villages have pubs
NONE of the villages has a supermarket
NEITHER Oreful NOR Angbridge has a cinema
Oreful has a church, SO does Clayford
Clayford has a car park, Angbridge ALSO/LIKEWISE
LIKE Angbridge and Clayford, Oreful has pubs
UNLIKE Oreful and Clayford, there are no churches in Angbridge.

Exercise

Make these sentences more elegant with appropriate contrast or similarity expressions:

- Jim and Marion live in a flat in Clayford. They are psychology students.
- Jim and Marion like jazz. They do not like rock music.
- They work hard during the university term. They relax during vacations.
- Last summer they went to Greece. Jim did not have much money. Marion did not have much money. They had a wonderful holiday.

2. *Cause, Effect and Purpose*

Look at this extract from Oreful's local newspaper, "The Oreful Gazette". It is not particularly well-written.

"The annual football match between Oreful and Angbridge was stopped yesterday after only ten minutes of play. Fighting started between the rivals supporters after our magnificent team scored the first goal, which the referee disallowed. The Angbridge supporters were drunk and the fighting soon became a riot and the police were called. They used tear gas. Shop windows were smashed. There were 34 arrests, mostly Angbridge supporters."

The CAUSE/EFFECT/PURPOSE elements in this text could be highlighted as follows:

CAUSE

The match was stopped *BECAUSE OF/DUE TO/* *ON ACCOUNT OF/OWING TO* fighting among the supporters	The match was stopped *BECAUSE/AS* fighting had started

EFFECT

The fighting became a riot *SO/THUS/THEREFORE* the police was called	Shop windows were broken This *LED TO/RESULTED IN/* *CAUSED/BROUGHT ABOUT* intervention by the police

PURPOSE

The police used tear gas *TO/IN ORDER TO/SO AS TO* stop the riot	The police used tear gas *SO THAT/IN ORDER THAT* the riot could be stopped

Exercise

Add an appropriate CAUSE/EFFECT/PURPOSE expression to make these sentences grammatically logical:

- *HE RAN FAST CATCH THE TRAIN*
- *SHE FELT ILL LAST WEEK JENNY DIDN'T GO TO WORK*
- *THE PETROL TANK WAS EMPTY. THE CAR STOPPED.*
- *SHE LIKED YOUNG PEOPLE. SHE DECIDED TO BECOME A TEACHER*
- *PASS HIS EXAMS TOM STUDIED HARD*

3. *Addition*

We use the notion of *ADDITION* when including an extra element in our argument to make it more emphatic.

For example:

"Astrology is not a scientific discipline. It lacks precision. No major philosopher considers it useful."

Whether we agree or not, we can strengthen this argument:

"Astrology is not a scientific discipline. It lacks precision.

IN ADDITION,
WHAT'S MORE,
FURTHERMORE,
MOREOVER,
BESIDES,
AS WELL AS THAT,

no major philosopher considers it useful."

Compound nouns

Compound nouns are another difficult obstacle for a French reader encountering a text in English. This difficulty derives mainly from the fact that attributive adjectives precede the noun they modify and do not change in gender or number.

A compound noun is said to be composed of at least three words, two of which are grammatically nouns.

Look at this (admittedly exaggeratedly-long) sentence:

"They designed a series of beautiful reinforced-concrete open-plan fifteen-storey prestige but low cost functional office buildings which they hope will attract business to the de-populated town." What does the sentence describe?

BUILDINGS

All the words preceding "buildings" may be described as "real" or "false" adjectives. With the exception of "but", each modifies the word "buildings", the principal noun in the sentence.

There are several things to be noted here:

- all the adjectives precede the noun
- some are "real" eg: "beautiful"
- others "false" eg : "prestige" or "office"
- although "buildings" is plural, none of the adjectives reflect this
- even "fifteen-storey" does not take an "s".

Now translate this sentence into French.

Exercise

Translate the following compound nouns:

- a single important stimulus point
- a proper language encoding process
- sequential sensory memory traces

- a conditioned response formula
- experimental personality research techniques

Modal verbs

The difficulties presented by modal or "defective" verbs are to be found not so much in their meaning (after all, their equivalents exist in French) but in their nuances. Perhaps the best way to look at this problem is to separate these verbs into their several "notional" contexts and deal with each in turn. The principal contexts are:

- OBLIGATION
- PROBABILITY
- PERMISSION

(As we shall see, some of these verbs exist in more than one context)

a) Degrees Of Obligation

To take an everyday theme:

Holidays in Thailand

- You MUST/HAVE TO buy a plane ticket
- You SHOULD/OUGHT TO be vaccinated
- You NEED TO take plenty of light clothes because of the humidity
- You CAN take a camera if you wish
- You do NOT HAVE TO/NEED TO change money in advance, as there are plenty of banks in Thailand
- You SHOULD NOT exchange money on the black market
- You MUST NOT forget your passport

b) Degrees of probability (or forecasting)

Read the following situation:

Municipal elections will take place next week in the village of Clayford. The mayor, Councillor George Chilcott has been in office for 19 years. He is popular with the older villagers, who think he will be re-elected without difficulty. But this year the election is complicated by a challenge from a younger councillor, Jenny Beckett.
Read this conversation, overheard in one of the pubs:

"Old George Chilcott WILL be re-elected, I'm sure." (1)
"I'm not so certain. That Jenny Beckett's very popular with the young people. She SHOULD get their vote easily." (2)
"Perhaps you're right. It COULD be a close contest." (3)
"Old George SHOULDN'T lose, I agree. After all, 19 years of service (4) to the village. People WON'T forget that in a hurry." (5)
"Another pint?"
"Yes, thanks." .../...

This conversation could also be written:

% of probability

positive	100 % 60 % 30 %-50 %	1) WILL - MUST / IS BOUND TO / WILL DEFINITELY BE 2) SHOULD - OUGHT TO / WILL PROBABLY / IS LIKELY TO 3) COULD - MAY/ MIGHT
negative	60 % 100 %	4) SHOULDN'T - OUGHT NOT TO 5) WON'T - WILL DEFINITELY NOT

c) *Permission*

Look at these mini-conversations, illustrating permission:

"CAN I open the window, please?"
"Go ahead."

"MAY I switch on the television?"
"I suppose you CAN, but for God's sake keep the sound down."
"COULD I turn left here, officer?"
"No, you CAN'T, madam. There's been an accident just up the road."

Exercise

Read the following - adapted - text, adding appropriate modal verbs in the blanks. (In many cases more than one verb is possible, but try to use a different one each time).

We __________ define what we mean by ability. But this definition __________ not always be consistent. A __________ be good with mechanical devices while B __________ be better at electronics. But to define ability __________ we have reliability of performance.
Furthermore, differences in performance __________ be explained by different levels of age or general intelligence. However, intelligence tests __________ be deceptive. Research is still in its infancy but psychologists __________ allow themselves some grounds for optimism in this field.

Achevé d'imprimer sur les presses de la SNEL S.A. – Rue Saint-Vincent 12 – B-4020 Liège
tél. 32(0)4 344 65 60 - fax 32(0)4 341 48 41– février 2004 – 31196

43653 - (II) - (0,8) - OSB 80 - EDIC - MMC – Dépôt légal : mars 2004
Dépôt légal de la 1re édition : 3e trimestre 1991

Imprimé en Belgique